Modern Fables

Praise for Marty Nemko's Previous Books

"The best of the best." *Warren Farrell, author of The Myth of Male Power.*

"The best career and possibly life advice you could ever give." *Dr. Mark Goulston, author of Just Listen who was Professor of Psychiatry, UCLA.*

"Here's the advice of a really smart person." *Michael Scriven, Past President, American Evaluation Association*

"It took my breath away... an enlightening compendium of innovative, resourceful, useful, out-of-the box articles. *Michael Edelstein, Past President, Association for Behavioral and Cognitive Therapy.*

"Incredible ratio of unique ideas per sentence." *Jonathan Wai, Research scientist, Duke University.*

"Magnificent food for thought, for this author is inventive, creative, and blazes wonderful, thoughtful, new trails for all of us." *Walter Block, Wirth Eminent Scholar, Loyola University, New Orleans.*

Dear Reader,

These fables attempt to provide life lessons without how-to articles' aridity and pontification.

I welcome feedback: mnemko@comcast.net.

About the Author

Marty Nemko holds a Ph.D in educational psychology from the University of California, Berkeley. He was called "career coach extraordinaire" by *U.S. News,* has worked with over 5,000 clients, and enjoys a 96% client-satisfaction rate. He is in his 28th year as host of *Work with Marty Nemko* on KALW-FM, a National Public Radio station in San Francisco. He has written over 3,000 articles, including many for *TIME, The Atlantic, the Washington Post, U.S. News*, and *Psychology Today*. This is his ninth book.

Table of Contents

Dedication

To my clients, readers, listeners, and my wife, Dr. Barbara Nemko who, for 40+ years, has put up with a husband who works 60+ hours a week.

People

Nice Guy

Tommy was always disliked because he was a know-it-all. He couldn't help it. He was smart and not restrained enough to hide it. So the kids hated him.

He tried to compensate by being ever so nice. He was so careful to not hurt anyone's feelings. He did all sorts of favors for kids, even though they were rarely reciprocated.

Indeed, the nicer he was, the more kids took him for a patsy. They felt fine about ignoring him, asking Tommy for more favors, and treating him insensitively, even cruelly. For example, as a pre-teen, he got chubby and the kids called him "Tits Tommy."

He responded as his parents taught him: "Turn the other cheek." Alas, that was seen as a sign of weakness. So the taunts grew into his getting beaten up often for some mock offense. "Why are you looking at my girlfriend?"

In high school, Tommy decided that the way to attract girls was to be really polite, tactful, buying them little presents, fully respectful of their sexual reticence. The popular girls saw that as unattractive. The only girl who liked him was Rita who, because she was very unattractive. was starving for kindness.

Despite his seeing, again and again, that being nicer than average results in *less* respect, he went through life being Mr. Nice Guy, clinging to the belief that it's worth the opprobrium in exchange for doing what's cosmically right.

Alas, even his wife and sons took advantage of him. The nicer he was, the more indifferent, indeed antipathic they were to him. He tried hard to please them but they, increasingly, with ever greater confidence, acted as though his wants were irrelevant.

So as Tommy aged, he grew ever more dispirited. "I just don't fit on this earth." Alas, unlike in the movies, he never met anyone who treasured him for his kindness. Nor was he rewarded by his employers or society.

He was nice even to the nurses who injected him with chemotherapy and then the euthanasia drug. Perhaps the only time he showed strength was in his will. He left most of his assets to charity.

The takeaway

People are more inclined to be nice if they've invested in you. That's why people play hard to get or are attracted to bad boys and bad girls–A person has to work to succeed in such relationships. Robert Cialdini, author of *Influence*, calls it *commitment bias*: We're more likely to give more to someone or a cause if we've already given.

That's why non-profits ask for only a tiny commitment at first, for example, your alma mater's alumni association invites you to the homecoming football game. Then they slowly ratchet-up The Ask until you've left them a boatload. Beware of getting manipulated.

Not withstanding all that, ideally, we'd all be willing to pay the price for living a life of kindness. Alas, that's a lot to ask.

Average Jane

In school, teachers focused on the brilliant and on the slow, so Jane was pretty much ignored.

Jane's classmates liked the good-looking kids and made fun of the ugly ones. They barely noticed average-looking Jane. At her 50th high school reunion, most people couldn't even recall who she was.

In college, while Jane wanted to date, she felt uncomfortable trying to stand out—being perky, dressing sexily, and so on. So she was pretty much ignored.

When Jane applied for jobs, her resume didn't stand out from the pile so the best she could get was a job as a rent-a-car reservationist, where she rarely chatted much with customers or co-workers. She was eminently forgettable.

Jane liked hiking and joined a MeetUp hiking group but even when she approached fellow hikers, the conversation quickly petered out and they'd move on.

Jane had some modest romantic relationships but sooner or later, they'd end it. When Jane asked for an explanation, the best they could come up with were things like, "There's nothing wrong with you. There's just not quite the spark."

Jane thought that perhaps she could be seen as special if she worked with disabled people, so she volunteered at a group home for people with intellectual disabilities. But she had difficulty helping them and got little recognition for her efforts, so after a few Saturdays, apologetically, she quit.

Next, she tried volunteering at an animal shelter. She and the doggies loved each other but it didn't feel enough. "Am I going to be ignored, not cared about by anyone except dogs and my parents who are now dead?"

At the end of her 50th high school reunion, she trudged back to her car, gently closed its door, and cried. Would she die unexceptional, unrecognized? She sat there for three hours trying to concoct a basis for hope. She considered dolling herself up, puffing herself up, bubbling herself up, but in the end decided that self-acceptance was the wisest course.

Jane spent her last decade in relative contentment by reading, gardening, hiking, painting, watching TV, petting dogs at the shelter, writing letters to the few people who had shown even modest interest in her, and volunteering at a suicide hotline.

A go-getter might have done more to improve her lot but Average Jane had just average drive. Many people have done worse.

What, if anything, might you have said to Jane?

Playing By The Rules

Decker had become a millionaire largely because he played by The Rules.

Yes, he could have a fancy car but it must look understated—silver Lexus, not red Corvette. His clothes need look inconspicuously expensive, for example, the tiny black-and-white word "Facconable" on the shirt, not the bright green Izod alligator.

Decker was tired at the end of his venture capitalist workday but The Rules deem visible fatigue (or any emotion other than mild pleasantness) unacceptable. So he took a deep breath, struggled out of his car, and turned his game demeanor back on for his second shift: the one at the club's bar.

That demeanor was well practiced—Of course, shoulders back, head slightly above 90 degrees to look confident but not pompous. No matter how tired you are, you must stride, not trudge but not so fast that you seem hurried. As the old commercial said, "Never let them see you sweat." Inside the bar, the stride must give way to a confident amble but certainly not the padding of an insecure wannabe. He had tried out dozens of smiles in front of the mirror until he settled on the one that appeared most natural and brought out the best in his facial features. And Decker practiced it until it was firmly in muscle memory and could be summoned on command.

On seeing his fellow denizens at the bar or in the clubby chairs, Decker nodded with that crafted smile, varying it just enough to avoid it appearing pasted. At this point, he could have approached them without paying the price of seeming too anxious but he preferred to slow his amble and slide to the bar, hoping someone would ask him to join them. The Rule is that the power resides in the recipient of the request, not in the requester.

Decker wouldn't even call the bartender even though she looking in the other direction and wasn't busy. Decker waited until she saw him. Thus, when she finally did, she might feel the need to apologize, whereupon Decker would graciously say, "Not a problem," all of which conveys to any onlookers that Decker was a gracious good egg. "I'd like a Beefeater Martini, please." The right drink, the right gin.

So, as usual, Decker had laid his foundation properly and as a result, before even his drink had arrived, Bill Oliver a fellow venture capitalist sidled up. All clubby types had read *How to Win Friends and Influence People* or one of its myriad derivatives, and knew to not talk business too quickly. So although they had not the slightest interest in each other's family, hobbies, and other innocuities, that was the requisite prattle for the first five minutes. Decker kept a list of the names of even casual acquaintances' spouse and kids' and their core interests, so he could toss off, for example, "Bill, I recall last time we spoke, you mentioned you were hoping Bradley would be getting into Choate. Any luck?" Decker would not, of course, say, "I recall you were trying to *pull strings* to get Bradley into Choate." That would violate The Rule against willfulness.

Decker and Bill were in the middle of their pre-deal dance when Decker's phone rang. "Would you excuse me a moment? It's my boss."

Decker ambled to a quiet spot and listened: "I'm so sorry to have to tell you this, Decker, but I wanted to let you know as soon the decision had been made. Decker, we've decided to go in a different direction."

Decker couldn't maintain his The Rules demeanor: "What do you mean, a different direction?! I've been an above-average performer. What is this about? . . .What do you mean you're looking for someone with a fresher approach? Are you firing me because I'm an older white male? No, you wouldn't admit that."

Decker then realized that his show of emotion could hurt the reference he'd get and perhaps his severance. So he mustered as much restraint as he could. "James, I'm sorry. Thank you for letting me know."

Decker couldn't muster an amble. He plodded back to Bill and simply said, "I need to go. We'll continue this next time." (Of course, Decker knew there well might not be a next time but The Rules prohibit such candor ...unless it's expedient.)

He drove home and told his wife who said all the right things, including telling him to "Feel free to take a week or so off to regain your bearings." (Internally, with him being the primary breadwinner supporting a lifestyle, including two kids in private school, she was nervous: "He's 50 and has only soft skills. Will he get a job without our having to dip into savings?"

But she never imagined what he ended up doing. Yes, he took a week to think about it all but his conclusion was unexpected—utterly: Decker entered an ashram and renounced all his worldly goods. I won't regale you with all the details. I'll merely let you know that when he did it, she divorced him. Oh, and I should tell you that he went onto the Berkeley campus with $100,000 in $100 bills, flung them all into the air and enjoyed the "anti-materialistic" Berkeley students swarming, diving, fighting for as many bills as they could grab.

After three months of meditating, chanting, and eating locally grown, sustainable organic vegetables over fair-traded brown rice, Decker was bored. Then one day, as he was shuffling around the ashram, (In an ashram, shuffling is The Rule), he noticed an unused utility room that faced a busy street. He got permission to open a bookstore and cafe there called The Town Hall Meeting Cafe. On the cafe's website, anyone could sign up to lead a one-hour discussion on any topic. Also, there were read-alouds for children, teens, adults, and seniors. Such events attracted a good number of customers who stayed a long time and thus often bought food and drink and occasionally, with the good will acquired, bought a book, even though they could use Amazon to peruse a far bigger selection at a far lower price. Decker ended up only netting $15 an hour but was much happier than as a venture capitalist.

His wife used part of the divorce settlement to get an MBA and then got hired by Decker's former employer.

*I read this **on YouTube.***

The Prudent Millionaire

Robert would always would rather save than spend. In the 1st grade, he had already started putting money into a piggy bank. In the 3rd grade, he opened a savings account. He loved watching the teller update his bankbook, seeing his balance increase and especially the red entry for interest. He was amazed that the bank would pay *him* for safekeeping his money.

Robert started taking after-school and summer jobs starting in the 7th grade. He saved most of what he earned, only occasionally buying, for example, firecrackers for July 4. And for those, he bargained hard, usually walking away to test if he had negotiated the lowest possible price.

To save his family money, Robert went to community college and then transferred for his bachelor's degree to the nearby public university, where he could live at home and, along with having taken a work-study job, be one of the rare students who graduated college with no student debt.

As an adult, Robert made a middle-class living as a librarian but remained unusually thrifty. He bought a studio condo in a "bad" neighborhood and furnished it from garage sales, Craiglist ads, and Ikea. He always drove an old, gas-stingy Toyota until it dropped. He bought his clothes at Wal-Mart or thrift stores. He mainly ate at home and economically: chicken, vegetables, tuna, fruit, etc., and when he ate out, mainly at hole-in-the-wall restaurants. He bought most other items on Amazon, which, because of its Marketplace, enabled him to get the lowest price from among many vendors. His vacations were driving rather than flying ones, and he stayed at airbnbs or low-cost motels.

He always paid the credit card bill in full, never paying a penny in interest. He invested 10% of his paycheck in his 401K and another 10% in the highest yielding bank CDs. (A master list is on Bankrate.com.) When he was dying, he left instructions that he be cremated and inexpensively: "No fol-de-rol."

So by the time Robert died, despite having earned only a librarian's income, his estate was worth $1.5 million. He thought about leaving it the National Association for Gifted Children, which lobbies for more money for under-served high-potential kids. But his friends and family said even the $1.5 million would be only a drop in most nonprofits' bucket, much would go to "administrative expenses," and, because gifted education is out of favor, would probably result in less benefit than if he left the money to family. He didn't quite agree but yielded to the pressure: He left his money to his brother and sister.

With the inheritance, his sister traded up to a larger house in a fancier neighborhood. His brother bought a Jaguar, added a recreation room to his home, and took his family on safari. He put the remaining inheritance in risky stocks. "After all, it's found money." As of this writing, he lost 40%.

And so went Robert's prudence.

Affirmative Actions

Lee's father worked horrendous hours in a restaurant. That, plus a desire to use his natural math and science ability to help humankind made Lee one of the few kids in high school who knew what he wanted to be when he grew up: a scientist. Lee even knew what he wanted to specialize in: infectious diseases, because a few of his relatives had died in China's 1946 bubonic plague epidemic.

Fueled by that and by an angry, Type A personality, Lee worked fervently to get top grades in high school and got into MIT. He continued to work tirelessly and got into U.C. Berkeley's prestigious PhD program in infectious diseases and vaccinology. Again, working prodigiously, even sometimes frantically, he had three journal articles published before he finished his degree. And there was no dabbling. All three articles were on his specialization: mutated bioweapons and vaccine creation.

So it was no surprise that Lee landed a tenure-track professorship, although his options were constrained because his wife got a great job offer in Dallas. So he took a position at Texas State University at Bluffview. She reassured him, "Hey, that's so close to Dallas's International Airport that we can easily travel anywhere."

Not surprisingly, Lee worked hard and well both at his teaching and research and so when it came time for his tenure review, he was confident. Alas, two professors came up for tenure in his department that year and for budget and political reasons, only one could be granted tenure. It was granted to the other person whom Lee deemed "vastly inferior," whom he believed got tenure for "non-merit reasons."

When a person doesn't get tenure, they lose their job: It's up or out. And so Lee was well aware that his career was likely doomed.

There are very few tenurable professorships, especially for people whose gender and race is "overrepresented." And because there are so many applicants wielding prestigious PhDs and even post-docs, he'd have a particularly hard time. He'd have to convince a university to hire someone who was denied tenure at the Texas State University at Bluffview.

During Lee's final semester, in one of his various efforts to deflect his fury, he experimented in his lab with creating mutated bioweapons, not that he planned to use them but it somehow felt good, in the way that some kids play sports to let off steam. Indeed, by the end of the semester, Lee had created vials-full of airborne, highly communicable mutated virus. And just to be safe, he created a vial of vaccine.

After his final semester was over, Lee was no calmer. Indeed, his anger grew. It hurt when had to walk his possessions out past the office of the professor who had gotten what he deeply felt was *his* tenure position. And he got angrier and angrier as the fears about his job prospects were confirmed.

Then, one day, before leaving home for his usual errands, he injected himself with the vaccine. Next, as usual, he stopped for gas, he went to the supermarket, but then he added the short ride to Dallas's international airport. He parked near the furthest shuttle-bus stop in the parking lot, taking his attaché case with him. When the full-sized bus arrived, he was first on and sat in the back, the least convenient seat so his release of the mutated bioweapon would be least likely to be noticed.

At each stop, the bus filled with more people. A minute before arriving at the terminal, he opened his attaché, its cover blocking anyone from seeing, and opened the Tupperware container, which released millions of the bioweapon viruses into the bus's air. By the time the bus arrived at the terminal, all the passengers had breathed more than enough to become fatally infected and would then infect countless people in the terminal, on the plane, and in all the cities and towns, worldwide, they were flying to.

Lee walked with the others into the terminal, then turned around, waited for the shuttle bus, returned to his car and went home.

By the time, first symptoms appeared 10 days later, those 30 passengers had flown all over the world and with each sneeze or cough had released communicable bioweapon. Within a month, millions of people were infected. Because the virus had been mutated, there was no vaccine. So most of them died. Infectious disease specialists couldn't even identify the outbreak's origin because people in many locales all around the world showed symptoms at essentially the same time.

As stories of the deaths and potential Armageddon dominated all thought, Lee's guilt grew and he told his wife that he was the cause. For a moment, her love for him made her hesitate but she then called the police, and he didn't try to stop her.

*I read this **on YouTube.***

Afterword: I have consulted with a former CIA operative who said that this scenario is the type that "keeps the CIA up at night." I am ignorant of how to manufacture or disperse bioweapons and deliberately have not even attempted here to guess how it could be done. So this story should pose no threat to the public, certainly far less than the hundreds of book-length novels--Amazon's Goodreads alone lists a top 100--plus the many non-fiction books and articles that have been written about bioterrorism.

Yield

 "Should I answer it or leave it blank. There's a penalty for wrong answers."

David was taking the SAT for the fourth time and his score had gradually risen from an already lofty 1420 to 1510. That met his goal: 99th percentile, which would boost his chances of getting into his dream school, Harvard.

In addition, David had completed the requisite absurdity of taking all Advanced Placement (college-level) courses in high school and killing himself to get nearly all A's at the expense of a social life. Too, he chose expeditious extracurriculars. For example, every college needs a tuba player and few applicants play the tuba. His application essay studiously trod the required line: balancing assertiveness and humility plus a safe foundational principle: urging more redistribution to women, minorities, and the poor.

Thus David got the thick envelope, which invited him to Visitas: "our April celebration for newly admitted students." Admissions weekends are more accurately but less appealingly described as yield boosters— Yield is the ratio of enrollees to admits. Even Harvard worries about losing admitted students to competing universities.

Visitas was thus filled with fun events as well as an invitation for admitted students to sample "selected" classes, that is, cherry-picked to be the most engaging. David decided to sample what wasn't selected. So he left the beehive of admitted students, who were bubbling in their superiority and visions of a Harvard diploma opening fantastic career doors. Instead, David wandered through classroom buildings, peeking into classes. Each one was more boring and irrelevant than even high school: formulas of stochastic processes, Derrida deconstruction of patriarchal literature, a proof of the Cayley-Hamilton Theorem, socioeconomic antecedents of the first Peloponnesian War, chiaroscuro use by Gerrit van Honthorst.

"This is what I worked so hard for? This is what I prostituted myself for, gave up my teenage years for?" David then sat under a tree, thought for what must have been an hour, then pulled out his phone and ordered an Uber. "Logan Airport, please."

David knew he'd not go to college, figuring that as a smart, hard working self-starter, the benefits of the diploma would be outweighed by his being able to hand-pick his learning opportunities and saving $300,000, which is the true full cost of four years at most selective private colleges. (Four years at a brand-name public costs, total sticker price, $200,000.) And many students take longer than four years to graduate. Plus, David liked that he would take charge of his life rather than toadying along the prescribed, boring, irrelevant, rite-of-passage path.

Nevertheless, David knew he had nothing to lose by, rather than turning down Harvard, deferring his admission for a year, which many colleges, including Harvard, allow. So he sent in the deferral form.

"But now what?" David enrolled in a top-rated Lynda.com course on entrepreneurship but felt isolated and so also enrolled in an honors American literature course at a community college. To see what it's really like to be a lawyer, he volunteered as a go-fer at his dad's law firm where he got to sit in on meetings and even ask questions. He applied for jobs as a personal assistant to a small business owner, figuring he'd learn a lot by seeing an entrepreneur in the real world. But the only person who would hire him, a mere high school graduate, was the owner of a one-person transmission shop who was longer on expedience than on ethics. Repulsed at seeing the owner spray paint a used transmission to make it appear rebuilt, David quit.

And in July, David felt no choice but...to yield. He wrote to Harvard's director of admission: "I would like to withdraw my request for deferred admission. I'm excited to, this fall, begin my studies at Harvard."

*I read this **on YouTube.***

Rapist

Kim is a psychotherapist in private practice and at night, teaches a college course: *Race, Class, and Gender in Psychotherapy.*

After class, Kim walks to the train through a dicey neighborhood. When she first started doing that walk, she would remind herself not to be hypocritical: that is, to not excessively worry about 'those people." And for 11 years, not a thing happened, but one night, a man jumped from the bushes and raped her.

Kim felt she should be strong and continue teaching the course the same way. She wasn't going to abandon her strongly held values merely because of one incident, no matter how devastating.

But should she continue walking to the train? "I'm tempted to take a cab to the train from now on. I'm scared. But should I capitulate to my irrational fears? I walked that route for 11 years without a problem. If I let exaggerated fears dominate me, I'd be doing what I urge my students not to do. No!"

The only change Kim would make would be to her private practice's website and business card. She didn't want to limit her practice to just women—She felt that would be sexist. But she would change how she described the kind of work she did so it would appeal more to women: spirituality, depression, and yes, issues around pregnancy and menopause.

And that worked. Almost all her prospective new clients were women. Then, one day she got a call from a man: "Hello, my name is Buck. I'm an ex-Marine and I want a therapist to help me see if I have a softer side. Will you work with me?" Kim was delighted and they made an appointment.

But all week, Kim was a bit nervous And when he walked in, she wasn't reassured. He wore a camouflage t-shirt emblazoned, "Warrior."

After offering Buck a glass of water, as much to calm herself as to slake his thirst, Kim asked, "So, what made you decide to explore your softer side?"

After a long pause, he said, "I raped a woman. I could tell you that it was a date and in the middle of making out, she changed her mind and I was drunk but that would be a lie. I'm an angry guy and I get crazy seeing all the reverse discrimination in the military, in college, when I was looking for a job, even on the commercials! So one night, I just took it all out on this butch woman who was walking down the street. Really, don't you think the system today screws men?!"

"Are you able to calm down or should we end the session?"

"I'll calm down."

Kim said to herself, "I'm scared of him. Besides, I'm not sure I can work with an anti-lesbian rapist." But she wasn't sure she wanted to discontinue because that might make him come after her. So she opened the door to his quitting: "What makes you think I'm the right person to help you?"

He responded, "I read in the newspaper that you got raped. I thought that would make you the perfect person."

She felt shocked, stalked, and thought, "I'm a lesbian feminist pacifist Leftist who's been raped. And he's a woman-hating, lesbian-hating, angry, ex-Marine rapist who sought me out because I was raped?! On one hand, I'm the worst possible counselor for him but just maybe I'm the best or at least am well-suited. And maybe we'll both grow from it. Or as likely, we'll grow even more polarized and maybe he'll actually assault me!

So she said, "Let's both take a week to think about it and then let's talk on the phone to see if we should schedule another appointment." Buck rose slowly, stared at Kim for what felt like an eternity, turned around, and slinked out.

What would you do?

One-Hit Wonder

His life peaked when his bubble-gum song, *Love is the Answer*, climbed the charts, reaching number 3 in 1964. Lots of photo shoots, a tour, adoring fans, media interviews, including by one sycophant who couldn't stop giggling. It was a crowning moment.

It was downhill from there. The sequel songs sounded the same and so never made it. So his gigs paid ever less, which meant he had to hire weaker back-up players, singers, and tech, which meant his shows got worse reviews. Unlike some stars did, he didn't spend more than he earned, indeed had a prudently invested nest egg but that too started to dissipate, so he moved to a modest apartment and sold his Mercedes for an older Toyota.

When the gigs sunk to bars that mainly did karaoke, he needed to take a day job. The best he could get was car salesman. The sales manager chose him because she knew that some customers would think it's cool to buy a from a former rock star, even a one-hit wonder. But he was a musician, not a salesman, and hated having to "close 'em and up-sell 'em" so after his first three months, he had sold a total of six cars and at a low profit margin, so he was fired. Next stop, bartender where during breaks he'd sing self-accompanied on the guitar. Not surprising, that environment and his fall led to his own drinking and smoking dope, ever more often.

One night, he got home from his job—It was 2:30 AM because the bar closed at 2—to hear a voicemail from that giggling reporter from long ago. She had heard that he had fallen on hard times and wondered if he'd be willing to be interviewed for an article—She was now working, or rather volunteering, for a music website. Although embarrassed at the thought of his descent being publicized, his hunger for a bit of the old acclaim prevailed.

She asked him, "Walk me through your life. Start with just the positive. What are your life's most pleasurable moments? Start at the very beginning."

I remember when I was five, seeing a sidewalk of light gray and then a block of it that was darker gray. I stepped on it and it made an imprint of my foot, and when I came back the next day, it was still there. I loved that.

I really loved my first slow dance. It was in the 5th grade in the basement of a friend's house, and the record player—they had 45s back then—kept playing *To Know Know Know You is to Love Love Love You* and I kept dancing with the same girl for what must have been an hour. It really did feel like heaven, like the song "Stairway to Heaven." No, not the Led Zeppelin one, the Neil Sedaka one.[1]

I remember when they gave me an IQ test. I was scared to death but when they called my mother to tell the results, they said my intelligence was way above average. That did more to make me feel good about myself than anything, even *Love is the Answer.*

It also really felt good when they asked me to sing The Star Spangled Banner at elementary school graduation.

From high school on, of course, the big thing was having that hit, but it was like a coke high: so awesome but short, and the crash is hard and long.

The takeaway

---

[1] https://www.youtube.com/watch?v=pRhQFSTOVrI

What have been your best moments? Any way to amplify their effects now? Any way to duplicate some version now?

Have you been living on a past accomplishment and should look for a new goal?

Have you been rationalizing inaction, wishing it were the good old days?

If you consider yourself a has-been, should you aim high yet again? Or focus on acceptance and just appreciate smaller wins?

Seeker

When Marie was seven, her parents sent her to a Catholic church's Sunday school, selected because it was longer on peace and love than on fire and brimstone. But one day, Marie asked her teacher, "If God is loving, how come we have to spend a long time burning in purgatory before we can go to heaven?" Marie didn't understand the teacher's answer. Instead, she worried.

In college, she had a Jewish boyfriend who, like most educated Jews, attend synagogue only twice a year, if that. She went with him one time and decided Judaism wasn't for her simply because services were two to three hours long, mainly in Hebrew.

After college, Marie took a yoga class. That got her into meditation but she felt that meditation mainly just gave her a nap. And when she read *Scientific American's* review of the literature on meditation's benefits[2] (they're unproven,) she stopped meditating.

Next, Marie took a Buddhism class and worked hard to be in the moment and to stand back and observe life's miseries as a way of insulating herself from them. But while both tenets were valuable, she felt her spirituality didn't fully reside there.

Then she joined a Unitarian church and loved its sense of community and the idealism they preached and seemed to practice. Yet, ultimately, she felt "Unitarianism is just liberal activism wrapped in spiritual garb."

---

[2] https://goo.gl/9d6ud8

Finally, she decided to return to a Catholic church and there she stayed. She no longer believed in purgatory and could no longer "buy the loving God canard" in the face of deadly earthquakes, hurricanes, and the long, painful death of her baby to cancer. But she enjoyed services and being involved in the church. Not only were the rituals comforting, she somehow felt that Catholics were her people. Also, she enjoyed being able to step out of her gray-area-filled life and hear sermons of relative black-and-white, good and evil, a reminder of the centrality of basic values such as kindness even if we don't always live by them.

The takeaway

Marie's spiritual landing place is different from many people's. But have you found yours? Do you even want one? If so, what might your next step be?

Norma

Norma graduated from Leviathan University with a major in psychology and $132,000 in student debt and ironically took a job as accounts receivable clerk in Leviathan's bursar's office.

Her job was, yes, to send dunning notices to students who were late in paying their student loans and to respond to in-person pleas for forbearance.

It pained Norma to see the endless line of graduates and dropouts who couldn't afford to pay. She thought back to when she was in high school and was seduced by Leviathan's marketing materials that implied that its graduates are likely to get a well-paying job and explicitly blaring that misleading statistic, "College graduates earn $1 million more."[3]

But her job was to get the alumni and dropouts to pay. So, to student after student, she said, "I'm sorry." And she emailed letter after letter, "Your account is past due. To avoid additional penalties that accrue when we send delinquent accounts to a collection agency, please remit the balance due within ten days."

---

[3] https://goo.gl/aKbMIZ

But there was a last straw. A student begged, "I want a job where I can make a difference but I'm saddled with all this debt so I had to take a job selling insurance. I'm not cut out for selling. I'm cut out for helping people. I've living with five roommates and I still can't afford both my rent and my student loan."

On impulse, Norma simply zeroed out the student's account and said, "Your student loan is now paid in full. Go make a difference." The student sputtered, "But, but..." Norma waved her away. "Just go."

It didn't take more than an hour before her boss came in. "Zeus (the computer program) just kicked out a file: Mary LeFleur. Yesterday, she had a balance of $107,955 and today it's zero?" Norma lied, "I have no idea. Must be a computer glitch."

That bought Norma a little time but she knew that even if she claimed it was a typing error, she'd be out of a job within a day or even go to jail. So she decided to do as much Robin-Hooding as she could in her remaining time.

The next person in line was a hulk who came to Leviathan on a football scholarship but after a year, was told there now were better players and he lost his scholarship. He told Norma, "If Leviathan hadn't given me the scholarship, I would have gone to community college. But now, I have a year's worth of credits that may not all transfer and I've made friends here at Leviathan. So I feel stuck. Is there any way you can spread out the payments?" Norma lied again: "I just found a technicality that forgives ex-scholarship athletes' tuition for four years. Congratulations."

At that moment, Norma's boss, who had been hiding within earshot, burst out, along with a police officer. "Norma, I can't believe you stole from the University." She retorted, "The university sells a defective, very expensive product to thousands of students every year— I just established a return policy." The student chimed, "That's right!"

Nevertheless, the officer handcuffed Norma and took her away. Norma never felt prouder.

The judge found Norma guilty but sentenced her to just 30 days of community service: providing financial-aid counseling to low- and moderate-income high school students.

What do you think of what Norma did? What, if any sentence would you impose? Why?

Conversion

This story addresses the tension among family, religion, biology, and principle.

Priscilla and her husband Zachary, an anesthesiologist, were members of Phyllis Schafly's Eagle Forum, which describes itself as "leading the pro-family movement."

They were so happy when, after much praying, Priscilla finally got pregnant and had her first child.

John was the perfect child. Not only did he sleep through the night early and get toilet trained in just a few days, he was sweet. He loved getting and giving affection. He was patient, sharing toys with the other children in the church's preschool.

Then one day, when Priscilla was picking John up from kindergarten, one of the other parents said, with just a hint of derision, "You know, John is *exceptionally* sweet." Priscilla's heart leaped. She thought, "Could he turn out gay? I didn't do anything to make him gay."

Right away, Priscilla took John to the toy store. "Would you like a GI Joe? He shook his head. "How about a truck?" "No." "Here's a great SuperSoaker water gun!" He turned away, looked around and picked up a stuffed dog. "Mommy, can I have him?" Priscilla said, "Not today, John" and she cried.

Throughout John's childhood, Priscilla and Zachary avoided the issue. Yes, they tried to get John into sports to no avail but mainly they just quietly hoped he'd grow out of it.

But in high school, they pried open John's diary and read that he fantasized about having a boyfriend. So they scuttled him to a "conversion therapist" to try to "make him a functioning heterosexual." John said, "Mommy, daddy, I'll try."

And John attended four sessions of visualizations, counseling, "social skills training" and even a week-long camp of "prayer and group support." But before the week was over, John was crying, inconsolable, begged to go home, and his parents reluctantly picked him up.

When it was time for college, not surprisingly, Priscilla and Zachary wanted John to go to a Christian college but John refused to apply. He insisted on going to a state university. His parents relented only if he promised to not only join but be active in Intervarsity, the evangelical Christian student organization.

John attended an Intervarsity meeting but felt as he did at the conversion camp: that he had to escape. So he did and instead joined the Lesbian, Gay, Bisexual, Transgender Alliance. Finally, he felt at home.

And like many students who vigorously flap their wings of freedom on leaving their parents' nest, John had an exciting sex life.

And he became HIV positive. He did not tell his parents. Surprising, even to him, his response was to begin treatments for sex change. He took the hormone replacement therapy and then had the sex-reassignment surgery.

Alas, in the recovery room, John had a severe stroke. The only movements he would ever make would be with his mouth and he would be in significant pain for the rest of his life.

Upon seeing John in the hospital room, Priscilla thought but did not say, "God punished him." Instead, she took Zachary's hand and, with the other hand, held John's hand and said, "Let us pray." John stared at her hand and then, struggling for breath, spat on it.

John's chin seemed to stiffen and he said, "I wish I lived in California...The Die with Dignity Act....And I want to die as a woman."

Anesthesiologist Zachary reached into his pocket and retrieved a syringe.

Psychic

Angela never thought her husband would leave her but he did.

Frantic, she sought advice from her mother, friends...and a psychic.

Angela approached the neon sign that read "Psychic," adorned by a crescent moon.

She rang the bell and was buzzed into a room with chairs covered with a white leopard-design fabric surrounding a round table with a tablecloth that extended to the floor. The walls bore velvet paintings, for example, of an eye in a triangle surrounded by stars. A velveteen curtain separated the reading room from what was behind. Soft new-age music completed the ambiance.

A minute passed. Theresa, the "psychic," made her clients wait so she wouldn't appear too eager, and to build clients' anticipation.

Finally, from behind the curtain, a grandmotherly woman in a peasant blouse and skirt emerged.

"Welcome, my child. I am Theresa. I'm glad you sought out an intuitive. We all have the gift; I've simply practiced for a long time. I'm not 100% right but I usually can help. (That makes the client feel like she's not getting hyped and also gives her an out when she makes an error.) Tell me what is troubling you?"

Angela said, "You knew I had a problem?" (Fact is, almost all first-time visitors to a psychic have a problem.)

"Of course, my child," replied Theresa.

"My husband Joe has left me. I want to know if he'll be coming back?"

Theresa noted that the question's wording suggests she wants him back. Confirming that, from her peripheral vision, Theresa noticed that Angela still wore her wedding ring. Theresa tucked away that information for later use.

Next, Theresa used other tactics to gather information and establish credibility. She turned down the lights, lighted incense, and intoned, "Angela, please close your eyes and concentrate on you, Joe, and your marriage." When Angela closed her eyes, Theresa looked her up and down and noted her appearance's fastidiousness.

After 30 seconds, Theresa asked Angela to open her eyes, That way, Angela could see Theresa's efforts to "connect with the spirits." Theresa then closed her eyes, scrunched up her face, and looked into the dark crystal ball on the table. Its electric cord was hidden under the ball and dropped through a hole in the table connected to a foot-controlled dimmer slider. After caressing the ball and making noises of concentration for a suitable time, Theresa slowly pushed the dimmer switch so the crystal ball illuminated, revealing a hazy, face-obscured image of two children, two adults, and two old people. (Somewhere in that assemblage, the client will see "a connection.") After a long 30 seconds, Theresa sighed as if exhausted from the ordeal. That helped make Angela believe that Theresa was doing something spiritual and the exhausted face suggested bad news was coming. And thus, when Theresa then gently smiled, Angela felt relieved.

Theresa began, "My dear, I have good news for you. I see Joe returning and staying with you but you will need to make some changes. (Theresa will only propose modest changes to keep Angela feeling good about herself and, in turn, Theresa.)

Theresa continued, "It's a little hazy (which buys her wiggle room) but I wonder if Joe is frustrated with your perfectionism." (inferred both from her appearance and that most men aren't as fastidious.)

If Angela said no in a tentative way, Theresa would blame her error on Angela. "Perhaps that's part of the problem, Angela: You were insensitive to Joe's frustrations with you." Or, if Theresa sensed that Angela was secure in dismissing perfectionism as a reason Joe left, Theresa still wouldn't apologize. She would immediately distract Angela by asking a question that required her to think, for example, "Now I want you to think hard about the time you sensed Joe was most unhappy with you." But in this case, Theresa guessed right and Angela said, "You're right. Every time we go out together, he's frustrated at how long it takes me to get ready."

Theresa tries to get Angela to provide more information without it casting Theresa's "psychic powers." into question. She again gives herself wiggle room: "Especially in a first session (portending the "need' for more sessions,) the messages can be vague, so you may need to help me a little." Angela, of course, agreed to help.

Theresa continued, "There's an important person involved in your problem (See how vague) whose name (Note that she didn't mention whether it's first or last name to double her chances) begins with S, or is it C?" Odds are, Theresa knows someone-- whether a relative, friend, or paramour--with a first or last name or nickname that starts with S or C.

Angela struggles to come up with a name and finally has to settle on, "Well, my grandfather is Sam."

Theresa responds, "Yes. That's it. How could Grandpa Sam be impacting all of this?" Theresa closes her eyes, pretending to be invoking the spirits but her real purpose is to allow silence that might push Angela to reveal something. Bingo: "Well, my husband has visited grandpa a couple times recently." Theresa says, with certitude, "Angela, you must visit Grandpa Sam. A clue will be revealed there."

On the off chance Angela knew no one whose first or last name began with an S or C, Theresa would say, "It's someone your husband knows but you don't. Let's go in a different direction." Or she might try, "I'm going to say the letters of the alphabet. The name will come clear. Now look me in the eye." When Theresa reaches a significant person's first letter, Angela's pupils will likely dilate or contract.

There's still time left in the session, so Theresa looked into her crystal ball and said, "I see a piece of jewelry given to you by a relative." Have any idea what relevance that might have? (Psychics know that most women have at least one piece of jewelry with emotional power.) As it happened, Angela said no. So Theresa tried another high-yield example that seems to be specific to Angela but is widely applicable: "I see an old memento from childhood: a book, a toy, something like that." Amazed, Angela said, "I've been sleeping with my childhood doll since Joe left!" This added to Theresa's credibility and also created an opening for Theresa to extract yet more information from Angela without appearing to do so: "So Angela, what significance might that doll have?" Angela said, "Maybe it reflects my desire for the playfulness of childhood?" Theresa, just using plain common sense, asked, "Is it possible that adding more playfulness to your relationship with Joe might resurrect it?" Angela said, "Maybe."

Next, Theresa dealt tarot cards in a ritualized way until a card came up that lent itself to a story that would support what Angela wants to hear. Theresa said, "Good: The High Priestess card, the Shekhina. That signals the inner divine within a woman. This is the clearest signal yet that your heart remains with Joe and his with yours. If the love within either of you were dead, this card would not have emerged."

There was still time left in the half hour, so Theresa "read" Angela's palm, looking for two long crossing lines--"Another clear sign he's coming back." (*Most* people have two long crossing lines.)

At the 28-minute mark, Theresa asked, "Do you want to summarize what you have learned?" Asking Angela to summarize builds Angela's investment in the "learning" and in Theresa the "psychic" and may yield more information for Theresa to use in a subsequent session.

Angela summarized, "You're confident Joe is coming back but that I'll need to work on my perfectionism, especially when it affects Joe and perhaps be more playful with him. And that I should see Grandpa Sam to perhaps learn other clues."

Then, Theresa intoned magisterially, "Very good" (Everyone likes to be affirmed.) "We are off to a good start." (More intimation that that additional sessions will be "required.")

Theresa then waited in hopes that Angela would ask to schedule a next session but she didn't, so Theresa said, authoritatively, "I want you to meditate on what you learned tonight, letting it all ferment and then we will (not "should") get together tomorrow to move you forward." (Who could be against moving forward?)

If Angela had responded enthusiastically, Theresa would have up-sold her: "You need a one-hour intensive." But Angela just said, Okay." so Theresa deferred the up-sell until the next session. Perhaps Theresa could even convince Angela to go for "the weekend retreat, which we reserve for only special clients."

Angela left skeptical but somehow glad she saw the "psychic," especially since Theresa predicted that she and Joe would get back together.

The takeaway

When we're vulnerable, we're subject to being taken advantage of. It's not just Theresa's fee, it's her ill-founded advice. Especially in tough times, we should rely on people we can trust: our respected relatives and friends and, perhaps most of all, the wise man or woman within ourselves. Ask yourself, "What would my best self do now?"

For more on how psychics "read" people, see The Full Facts Book on Cold Reading[4] by Ian Rowland.

Unhinged

On Mar, 11, 2011, in his cottage on a remote part of coastal Sendai, Japan, old Hitoshi was, as usual, sorting stamps. Each had been placed in priority order in a glass tower. Each time he wanted to review one, he pushed a button and the next one was released.

He bought only mint, never-hinged stamps but additionally they had to be:

- Color precisely as in the catalog, no fading and of course no stains
- Crisp printing: Any waviness is the result of the stamp having been printed using worn plates
- No creases
- No inclusions in the paper stock
- Equal-sized margins
- All perforations intact, each of equal length, none bent.
- No dents in the stamp, for example, from the perforation machine
- Perfect gum: fully and evenly covering the stamp's back.

Hitoshi estimated that he had evaluated 3,000,000 stamps. He never touched a stamp with his fingers to avoid his skin oils touching the stamps and increasing risk of creasing a corner. Instead, he used special stamp tongs. While such tongs are available for a few dollars, he chose to spend $300 to get a custom-made one to perfectly fit his fingers, shaped into a semi-

---

[4] https://goo.gl/tRmPX7

rounded spade shape, with one end a little slimmer, the insides polished with ultra-fine steel wool and then plated in medical-quality stainless steel to ensure smoothness.

Perhaps not surprising, Hitoshi was as careful with everything. Because Japan is subject to earthquakes, everything was quake-proofed down to each cup in his cupboard, which were spring-attached to the wall. He takes a pill three times a day so he carried a timer around with him at all times set to go off at precisely 10, 5, and 12. Because he hated noise, he triple-glazed and soundproofed his house using special material he imported from Germany—superinsulation in the ceiling crawlspace and soundproofing strips around every window and door.

Suddenly, his normally pacific old Akita dog, Daisuke, which means "Great Helper," pawed his arthritic paw against Hitoshi. Moments later, the cottage started to shake, scattering all the stamps onto the floor.

Hitoshi glanced over to the stamps but decided to put Daisuke on a leash and the two of them limped under the mattress, above the box spring, the safest place in his house, something he had carefully selected years earlier.

When the shaking stopped, Hitoshi carefully left the bed, smoothed the bed's comforter, and let Daisuke off the leash. He returned to his stamps and methodically began replacing the stamps in priority order.

Minutes later, Daisuke starting limping toward the window, more quickly than usual and barking at its curtain. Hitoshi carefully rose from his table so the stamps wouldn't be disturbed, and tiptoed to the window, taking care to not step on any of the cracks between the floor tiles.

When Hitoshi arrived at the window, he carefully pulled back each of the two curtain panels so symmetry was retained. There, he saw a tsunami wave just yards from his house. He'd have only seconds before it invaded his cottage.

That moved even the deliberative Hitoshi into action. He raised the first of his 17 four-inch-thick stamp albums to the highest shelf but then the wall of water crashed the door and swept Hitoshi, Daisuke, and the stamp tower to the floor. The next victims were the stamp albums, each meticulously filled with thousands of rare, mint, never hinged, and otherwise perfect stamps, each stamp protected by its own plastic sleeve.

Two more waves, each smaller but still reaching the cottage, fortunately did little additional damage. And then it stopped, and the water started to slowly drain. Hitoshi could merely stare and didn't notice Daisuke convulsing on the floor behind him until the dog groaned. He bent down to his Daisuke, petting her to try to stop the convulsions but they wouldn't.

Hitoshi picked up the phone to call the vet but the earthquake and tsunami had knocked out phone service. He put Daisuke on the leash but she would not move so he carried the 40-pound dog into the car but the waterlogged vehicle would not start.

Hitoshi removed Daisuke and tried to get her to walk with him toward the vet's home/office a mile away. But the dog would not move, so Hitoshi carried the still convulsing dog. Every half-minute, the old Hitoshi would have to stop, put Daisuke down and try to get her to walk, but to no avail. After a half mile, Daisuke died.

Hitoshi stared at his only friend, started to cry, turned around, and trudged back toward his cottage. Then he noticed the only house on the way home, a shack, which appeared destroyed by the tsunami. He plodded there as fast as he could limp.

He knocked. No one answered. He nursed the askewed door and heard moaning. An old woman was trapped under a timber Her head was bleeding, profusely, her skin pale, eyes vacant.

Abandoning his usual meticulousness, he grabbed the only piece of cloth he could see that wasn't water-soaked and pressed it against the mortal wound. He tried to lift the timber off her to no avail. He said, "I'll get help."

"No," she replied weakly.

He continued to the door.

She: No, please. I was done before. This just helps.

He turned to her and she held out her hand. He took it. Then there was silence for what must have been a minute.

She: It's no longer fun...

He nodded.

She: I'd paint for a bit. Dance for a bit. Grow flowers for a bit. Flirt for a bit, well more than a bit.

He smiled.

She: I worked some too, helping orphans find homes, setting up museum exhibits, even running a geisha house.... Have you lived well?

And she died.

He stared at her, covered her head, bowed, and padded out and back towards his cottage. There, he mailed, unsorted, a handful at a time, of his now-damaged stamps to the people who'd still value them: his beginning stamp-collector customers.

Then he strode to his medicine cabinet, not caring whether he stepped on a gap between the tiles, and opened the bottle of the OCD medication he had heretofore refused to take. Next, he began cleaning his cottage, adequately but not perfectly, his furrowed brow relaxed.

Looking Out

Rebecca's first memory was of fear. She swears that she recalls at age 3, her mother saying she needed to call the doctor. Rebecca was terrified, picturing a needle.

At school, Rebecca was always afraid someone would make fun of her or beat her up, so she was very quiet.

At night, as early as age 10, she'd lie in bed thinking of how her life was "getting used up: I've already used up 1/7 of my life."

In junior high school, her heart pounded every first day of class, scared she wasn't smart enough or that the teacher wouldn't like her. So she said little, was eminently forgettable.

She refused to learn to swim, terrified she'd drown. Even a patient swim teacher had to finally tell her mom, "Maybe she's not quite ready to learn to swim." Her mom finally gave up when Rebecca was 14.

In high school, even though boys wanted to date her, she refused in fear of having to take her bra off in front of a boy.

The TV news scared her. For example, when the broadcaster would talk about a flu epidemic, she was scared she'd catch the flu and die. Imagine how scared she was when she came down with the flu while on a cruise ship with her parents and had to stay in the ship's infirmary for the cruise's remaining three days.

She refused to go away to college. It was simply too new, too alone. So she lived with her parents and went to the local college.

After graduation, scared of failing, the only jobs she sought were fail-proof ones: pizza delivery driver, retail sales clerk, housecleaner.

She married the owner of one of the houses she cleaned. Afraid of being pregnant and of delivering a baby, she and her husband adopted two kids. She quit work and became fully devoted, over-devoted, to caring for her kids. When, for example, her toddler reached out to pet a sweet little dog, Rebecca screamed, one of the earliest ways she transmitted her fearfulness to her children.

At age 40, Rebecca developed appendicitis and needed emergency surgery. Terrified, as they walked her to her pre-surgery bed, she fainted—pure anxiety.

At age 50, her childhood-rooted fear of death reemerged and she obsessed about it, reading every book on death and dying, from Christian, Buddhist, Hindu, philosophical, and psychological perspectives. Then lots of psychotherapy. Nothing worked. The more she thought about death and especially dying, the greater her fear became. Not surprisingly, her fear translated into hyper-vigilance about physical sensations. She catastrophized many sensations as a sign of cancer or heart disease. So she would often run to the doctor to get it checked out. Two primary-care physicians pawned her off: "Rebecca, perhaps you'd be better served by another physician or maybe a physician assistant—they have the time to be more thorough."

At age 65, Rebecca had a mild heart attack, and of course, was terrified thereafter in fear of another one. Her doctor had to put her on anti-anxiety medication, long-term.

She had few friends and when her husband died suddenly, she was alone with little to distract her from her fears.

Finally, at age 70, while watching TV, she saw a commercial recruiting volunteers for a local after-school tutoring program. She decided to volunteer. She found that her tutoring hours were her only worry-free ones—she was too busy worrying about her students. And so she filled her life with voluntarism. She worked five afternoons a week at the tutoring center. In the evenings, she read aloud to the blind. On weekends, she was a volunteer minister at her church, consoling the sad, sick, and bereaved.

While Rebecca still had moments of fear, she was largely cured by turning her attention outward.

"A Person of Substance"

A review of 18 studies[5] found that obese newborns are more likely to become obese adults.

So it was not surprising that Letitia, who was born weighing 9.7 pounds, would, at age 15, weigh 240.

Contrary to the stereotype of teens being mean, most of her peers were careful, never calling her "fat." A couple of kids called her what some fat-acceptance activists suggest: "a person of substance."

But privately, Letitia considered herself a pig. That was even though she ate less than one might think. Yes, occasionally, in frustration with her self-hatred and lack of friends let alone flirtations, she would overeat. But that didn't begin to explain her obesity.

Like many teens, in an attempt to form an identity, she started getting tattoos. People politely praised them, as we often do when someone does something edgy. Letitia rarely was praised, which motivated her to get more tattoos until she had covered both arms.

---

[5] https://goo.gl/VeVX7f

Letitia tried diets, first on her own. She'd be "really good" for a day or even a few days and lose a pound or two, but one few-minute "cheat" would negate many hours of being good. So she figured she needed to try a structured program. *Consumer Reports* rated Weight Watchers the best, so she tried that but soon quit because she found the rules too cumbersome and the weekly weigh-ins embarrassing, not only because of her weight and slow progress but because she was the youngest person there. Then she tried a medically supervised plan and, with great effort, lost 20 pounds in six months. But the thought of a lifetime of such restraint and, as she aged, a slower metabolism that would make it even harder, led her to despondency: "Shopping at Lane Bryant at age 16. I hate it." She began eating moderately. "Fat acceptance feels wrong but I don't feel I have a choice."

Her replacing weight-loss efforts with eating moderately allowed her to turn her focus to other things. Notably, she loved singing but hadn't allowed herself to get serious about it because she felt, as a "pig," she didn't deserve to. But now, she took singing lessons and with her teacher's encouragement, sang at a karaoke bar. At first, her voice kept cracking but eventually, she sounded good and got applause. "I've never been applauded about anything. It gives me goose bumps and makes me cry."

That gave Letitia the confidence to pursue a career. She was never good at school, not because of psychological issues associated with her weight, but because she simply found school hard. She was diligent enough—Indeed doing homework was a socially acceptable way to avoid trying to have a social life. She said, "School just isn't my thing."

So after graduating from high school, Letitia took a job at Lane Bryant as a sales clerk specializing in younger customers. She did well and within a year, received two promotions: to assistant store manager and then associate store manager.

At age 38, now 285 pounds, her doctor encouraged her to pursue weight-loss surgery and she looked into it. But the risks scared her too much and chose to accept the health and social risks of morbid obesity over the surgery. Instead, she started using a top-rated weight-loss app, My Fitness Pal, [6]and it's helping, albeit modestly.

Letitia, now 40, works as a sales manager in Lane Bryant's corporate office, hiring, training, and supervising retail sales people. Some weekends, she still sings at karaoke bars and even occasionally at a nightclub's open-mic night. She's still healthy and grateful for every day. All in all, she feels she's done okay.

Terror

It's October 10, 2015. As usual, Miriam woke up not refreshed-- She usually has trouble sleeping. Each morning, she's grateful for the first few minutes when her anxiety hasn't yet taken over her.

But within minutes, she starts to worry: that her kids won't have time enough for a good breakfast, that her anxiety is making her a bad wife, that that headache is cancer.

Miriam's husband reassures her yet again: "You've been to the doctor and she says you're just fine. It's anxiety. Take your Prozac and use your Pacifica app.[7] And that vigorous walk across the Damascus Gate plaza will de-stress you. I love you. I'll see you tonight."

She walks her two kids to school, worrying, excessively worrying, about a terrorist attack, especially as she gets to the plaza. After all, there had been recent attacks there and just since September 15,[8] Israel has suffered 117 stabbings, 41 shootings, and 23 car rammings.

At the school, Miriam kisses her children good-bye but doesn't leave until she sees them enter the building. Even their young faces show that they have absorbed their mother's angst. They seem to have already surrendered their childhood innocence to adult worries. After all, they sense that adults' attempt to live as though things are normal is just a veneer covering relentless fear. The kids' worry is reinforced by their Ashkelon relatives' phone

---

[6] https://goo.gl/rzLG6F
[7] https://goo.gl/W8Xmqx
[8] https://goo.gl/cfbEng

calls about having been <u>rained on by Gazan rockets</u>[9] and that her cousin once had to be hospitalized for shock.

Miriam arrives at the hotel coffee shop she manages and says hello to the security guard, who pats down customers before they're allowed in. That security effort doesn't reflect Rebecca's anxiety disorder. It's the norm in Israeli coffee shops, restaurants, and nightclubs that can afford a security guard.

Miriam leaves work daily at 3 so she can pick up her kids from school. Today, she gives them their weekly treat: a stop at a falafel café on the way home. As usual, she tells her kids to eat quickly—She can't stop thinking of all the suicide bombers who deliberately choose places where Israelis go for a bit of respite: <u>cafés</u>, <u>nightclubs</u>, <u>buses</u>, <u>hotels</u>,[10] even <u>bar-mitzvahs</u>.[11] Rationally, Rebecca knows that the chances of an attack are small but her anxiety disorder, by definition, trumps rationality.

After finishing, Miriam and her kids walk back across the Damascus Gate plaza when, suddenly, they hear screaming. <u>A 16-year-old is stabbing two old, screaming Jewish men</u>.[12] The police race to stop it but the terrorist tries to attack them, <u>screaming "Allah Akhbar"</u>[13] at which point an officer shoot him. Palestinians swarm the scene, "<u>rioting and throwing rocks at police</u>."[14]

Miriam swooned. "Mommy, what's wrong? What's wrong?!" Miriam started to cry and then so did their children. Passersby rushed to her aid as did a police officer. The embarrassment shocked Miriam into enough of a recovery to say, "I'm fine. It was just difficult to watch." She took her children by the hand and sped toward home. As soon as she was out of the onlookers' sight, she said, "Let's run." When they entered the apartment, she triple-locked the door and pulled out her Pacifica app.

Miriam told her husband that she can no longer take the stress and needed to quit her job. Her husband tried to change her

---

[9] https://goo.gl/cloeVm
[10] https://goo.gl/hNdKnH
[11] https://goo.gl/F1bJBr
[12] https://goo.gl/0FLGZF
[13] http://www.timesofisrael.com/woman-lightly-wounded-in-jerusalem-bus-stabbing/
[14] https://goo.gl/UNTkQF

mind: "All of us must continue to live. We can't let them stop us from living." Reluctantly, Rebecca agreed to continue working.

But on November 10, there were three separate terrorist stabbings in Jerusalem.[15] Miriam asked her boss for a week off, got it, and a week later decided to try to be strong, and went back to work.

Alas, on Feb. 3, 2016 at 2 PM, just an hour before Miriam would have been walking past the Damascus Gate with her children, police officers asked three nervous-looking young Arabs for identification. It turned out they were hiding machine guns, pipe bombs, and knives. The terrorists stabbed one of the officers to death and shot the other one to death.[16] Both officers were female.

Miriam quit her job and is scared to look for another. Her husband and children don't know how to handle it all. She has found a cognitive-behavioral therapist, takes her Prozac religiously, and practices desensitization and other activities with the Pacifica app.

Of course, there are explanations or at least rationalizations for violence on both sides of the Israel-Palestinian dispute, indeed most disputes.

But the human toll even on people who were not hurt or killed can be profound, especially if you have a predisposing emotional condition such as generalized anxiety disorder.

The takeaway

What should you accept or not accept about your limitations? It might be worth looking at the major aspects of your life: your career, relationships, physical and mental health, appearance, recreations, habits. Have you been beating yourself up about something you should finally make a concerted effort to change or accept as immutable so you can focus on something more productive?

---

[15] https://goo.gl/uSZCik
[16] https://goo.gl/8GiBtf

The Bar Mitzvah

I am a judgmental person and I'm proud of it, except when I'm not. For example, let me show you how judgmental I was at my nephew's bar-mitzvah today. Do you think I'm too judgmental or, rather, showing discernment?

I hate sitting in temple—Services are endless, hours of mainly Hebrew muttering in praise of an omniscient, omnipotent, benevolent deity. How could there be such a God if zillions of babies are born with agonizing diseases and then die leaving parents bereft. But I'd pay too big a price for not going to the bar-mitzvah. (sigh.).

I stared at Eli up there. He's barely shaving and is the kind of kid who, at the reception, would pour sugar into a soda bottle, shake it up, and spray it around. Because he's 13, he's now a man?

Eli has better things to do with his time than learning the haftorah (chanting a long Bible portion in Hebrew). On the other hand, the bar-mitzvah's other rite of passage, the drosh (creating and delivering a sermon,) is a great learning experience.

Finally, after an hour and a half of the rabbi and cantor droning, mainly in Hebrew, which, for an active 13-year-old, must feel like three hours—lanky Eli gawked his way up to the podium, like a condemned bourgeois to the French-Revolution gallows.

Maybe because it's been so long since I was bar-mitzvahed, I was amazed at how calm Eli seemed, although he was robotic. It's like the rabbi drilled and drilled him, drilled and killed him, until you could wind Eli up, press the button, and he'd deliver the haftorah. But—and here's a rabbinic secret—the rabbi can expand or contract the haftorah and drosh so, with effort, any kid can do it. Eli had the misfortune of being smart and hard-working, so the rabbi made him eat the whole challah: full haftorah chanted not read and a drosh he wasn't allowed to read nor memorize. He had to ad-lib it, aided only by a cheat sheet.

After Eli completed that feat, it felt anti-climatic that instead of applause, the rabbi acted as though Eli had done nothing, and just continued on with the mainly Hebrew droning. Another 45 minutes of that. No wonder synagogue attendance is down.

Of course, afterwards, there were the congratulations, in this case deserved, but I remember other bar-mitzvahs in which the kid was terrible yet polite society requires gushing, even though that reinforces laziness: "Even if I suck, they'll praise me." Grade inflation extends well beyond the classroom.

The grade inflation continues at the reception, a five- or even six-figure bacchanal in which, except for the size-2 wraiths, everyone eats their required minimum daily allowance in one meal. And there's Vegas-like entertainment: magic show, DJ, and/or hoo-hah band. All in honor of the kid becoming a far from true man. Mustn't that contribute to inflated sense of self, of entitlement to hyper-materialistic reward and being fawned over for something every Jewish kid gets merely because the calendar's pages have flipped enough?[17] Isn't that also true of weddings? Absolutely anyone can commit to an often untrue lifetime of "for richer, for poorer, in sickness and in health."

And how odd that, with each person developing an a different rate, the Jews (and Christians for confirmation) pick a single year—in early-teenhood no less—as when a kid becomes an adult. Haven't they read the books that say that kids brains' especially boys, aren't fully developed until their 20s? And one size doesn't fit all: Some teenagers act like adults while other people go to their graves childish.

On the dance floor, many of the women look like they're having an orgasm, the men a root canal. Then there are the men who sit bolted to their chair to avoid said root canal, even if people whisper about them.

Four, five, even six hours later, the blowout blows out—usually capstoned by yet one more monument to excess, for example, handing each departing guest a doggie bag with bagels and cream cheese in case the previous zillion calories aren't enough to preclude an early-morning carb and fat fest.

---

[17] Doing the haftorah and drosh are merely tradition. A boy or girl gets bar- or bat-mitzvahed merely by turning 13.

I drove home from Eli's bar-mitzvah, alternately feeling superior for my discerning values and hating myself for being so judgmental. Which do you think I am?

The takeaway

Today, "judgmental" is an epithet. And sometimes, that's deserved. But among my clients and friends, I've seen people be ever more reluctant to judge That's lamentable because judgment, discernment, is core to wise decision-making, indeed to improving society .

So, do you think you're too judgmental? Not judgmental enough? Is that true in general or with regard to some specific? Is there anything you want to change?

Depression

She, 28, is a cutter. "It's the only thing that can distract me from the psychological pain, which is worse."

Her pain comes from within. Externally, she comes from privilege. Both parents are professors and she graduated from Stanford with no debt. Her parents are patient with her depression, even when she reaches bottom and they must help her eat and get dressed.

She had always felt sad at her core, and in college attempted to tamp it down by staying busy: studying hard, joining clubs, dating, activism, plus adventure travel during the summers. But there was always the fear that, like a panther hiding behind a tree, her darkness would pounce on her.

Oddly, the pounce was triggered not by trauma—like a breakup or a parent dying—but from winning a dance competition. That brought into relief what, for her was, "the meaningless of it all."

Theresa's Stanford diploma got her hired as a poverty-program researcher for a government contractor but her depression soon got her fired. "I'm tempted to sue them under the Americans with Disabilities Act but I can't muster the energy."

The only job she has been able to hold onto is driving an ice cream truck, one of those that plays a jingle to bring out the kids, like the

Pied Piper. The routine, the structure, and that repeating melody comforted her. No one seemed to notice that, as when she was a dancer, no matter the summer heat, she wore long sleeves to cover her cuts, which extended all the way to her elbows.

Exacerbating the depression is her awareness that she isn't living up to her potential. When she is feeling good enough to care, she deplores herself.

Theresa craves love but nonetheless feels she can't expect to get it except from her parents. Indeed, her mother stopped her career in part to be there for her. When she emerged from her first major depressive episode, she found herself rushing into intimate relationships. Her urgency to get deep fast scared away all but desperate men.

When she finally fell in love with someone she respected, she soon pulled back: "I don't want him to see me like this and I don't want to bring him down." Following that deep disappointment, she shrunk her world ever more, rarely leaving her parents' house. She felt "I couldn't stop myself from choking-off my ability to feel. It's like part of me is an invasive vine that slowly chokes me."

Fortunately, she was able to make herself keep seeing her psychopharmacologist until she found an antidepressant that worked well enough to justify the side effects and to change dosage and/or medication when side effects were too severe or the benefits were wearing thin. Similarly, she tried-out psychotherapists until she found one she liked: someone smart and engaged, who balanced cognitive-behavioral with insight therapy, who recognized that she wanted homework but would only do assignments that were easier than one might expect a Stanford graduate to want.

She believes she may need psychotherapy and certainly anti-depressant medication for the rest of her life. She hates those constant reminders of her disease but recognizes that, while they won't cure her, "My last breakdown was so scary, I need to reduce their depth."[1]

She recognizes that she must do her part. She has to exercise daily and take her pill. When she senses herself going down, she has to strike the balance between accepting that her depression is causing it, which is largely beyond her control, while also gently trying to push herself up through the haze by making herself do basic tasks and by whispering to herself the reassuring message that this will pass. She even finds it helpful to try to be amused by the absurdity of it all.

Perhaps surprisingly, she has a love-hate relationship with her depression. Of course, she hates the deep dives but feels her depression makes her look at life more realistically and profoundly than do most normal people. She even believes that she has derived a benefit from having fallen into an abyss of such pain that it sapped her energy even to commit suicide, which at that point was her greatest wish. The benefit? That she is better able to appreciate the simple pleasures that many normal people don't: the first bite of a croissant, the broad softness of a rose petal, the puff of white in the azure sky.

Collaborator

This first part is not fiction. It's a paraphrase of a conversation I heard today on my daily hike around the lake I'll make up the conversants' names:

Jen: I lost 30 pounds on cardio. Want to sign up with me for the program? It's only $1490 and they give you lots of support.

Kat: Sounds like fun.

Jen: I don't know about fun but I lost 30 pounds.

Kat: I'd like to lose weight too. Maybe we should ask Madison if she wants to do it with us?

Jen: Sure.

Kat: I can't wait to go to the concert.

Jen: Me too. The hotel we'll be staying at is so cute.

Kat: Yeah. I'll bring a gallon of Ketel.

Jen: I'll bring $40 for drinks at the concert and $100 for gambling.

Kat: That sounds about right. Totally fun!

Jen: Hey, you want to take a day off to go to the Giants game?

Kat: Sure!

From here, it's a fictional account of Jen's life story.

As a child, Jen was always one of the "in" kids—She made sure she was: She wore the right clothes, talked about the right pop culture, used the right argot, for example, "She was all like, 'Are you mad at me?' and I was like, 'No way!'"

Much of Jen's time was spent in groups: at recess, sleepovers, shopping at the mall.

She chose her college mainly because most of her friends were going there.

She joined a sorority and welcomed the shared rituals and built-in group with whom she had a common bond.

After college, she applied for jobs for which the recruitment ad stressed collaboration, teamwork. She loved phrases like, "There's no I in 'team'" and was grateful when, occasionally, someone would pick up the slack for her. And it didn't bother her that team-decision-making meant that it took a long time to get things done and that those consensus-based solutions usually were tepid—that which everyone could agree on.

Unconsciously, Jen wanted to keep to The Schedule: date a lot until her late 20s, then find a husband, work until she had a baby and then stay home or maybe work part-time—like most of her friends.

And thus went most of Jen's collaborative life—including a bevy of friends helping her through her breast cancer treatments...and at her deathbed. Her room was filled with flowers, cards, and people were always visiting. Near the end, they all decided to throw her a final "party:" 20 of her BFFs were in the room, holding her hand, hugging her, telling stories about all the fun they had. Jen told the most.

Then, one of the visitors innocently asked Jen, "You've been so much a part of us. Who are you, yourself?" Jen, normally talkative, fell silent, thinking and thinking. After 20 seconds, someone could no longer stand the silence and said, "Well, I remember when Jen, Taylor, Chrissie, and I...."

When they left, Jen thought, "I benefited a lot from always being part of The Group but did the benefits to me and to others outweigh the liabilities?"

The takeaway

Are you primarily a collaborator? Has any loss of individuality been worth it? Is there something you'd like to do to be more individualistic? Group-oriented?

Procrastinator

Chad loved pleasure. As a child, he would do his homework as quickly as he could get away with so he could play sports, watch TV, or play video games.

In high school, when assignments got longer, he'd procrastinate until the last minute and, thanks to grade inflation, still got okay grades. That reinforced his procrastination—He knew the adrenaline rush would help him get it done—adrenaline addiction.

Chad got into the University of California, Santa Barbara, which his parents thought was more selective than it is, and Chad knew was a helluva party school.

Chad's procrastination worsened in college with the temptations of being away from parents' watchful eye. He majored in partying and minored in sociology because he thought that would be the easiest path out. Nevertheless, it took Chad six years to graduate, much to his parent's personal and economic chagrin.

Chad didn't pursue internships in college and, after graduation, avoided looking for a job, in part because it felt painful and he felt like an imposter: "What value could I possibly add?"

Finally he landed a job as a coordinator at a fashion-forward outdoorwear company. But even though that workplace was as laid-back as corporations get, his brinksmanship got him "laid off."

But Chad knew how to play and so attracted lots of women. Knowing he'd probably have a hard time making a good living, when he decided to settle down, he looked for "babes with bucks" and indeed found one, Heather, to marry him. After all, Chad was "super fun," motorcycle and all.

The honeymoon lasted until Heather got pregnant and felt she'd want to take at least a few years to stay home with the baby. Chad had been working sporadically, mainly through temp agencies as an admin but nothing that suggested he'd consistently make a middle-class income. So Heather started, gently at first, "encouraging" him to make greater efforts to find a stable, middle-income job. While Chad made some efforts—including hitting up his many friends—when they didn't "have anything for him," he started drinking more and doing more pot, which only decreased his motivation further, a vicious cycle.

Heather's encouragement devolved into nagging and fights, including screaming matches in front of their newborn. Chad "couldn't deal" and so initiated divorce. Heather was fed up with him anyway so they divorced without a protracted legal war.

After six months with the baby, Heather knew she needed to get back to work and did. Meanwhile, Chad is back living with his parents, playing lots of video games, visiting his son less often than he should, and claiming to be looking for a job.

His father said to him,

Chad, some people have to reach rock-bottom before they change their procrastinating ways. Others prefer to stay at rock-bottom, either because of—as psychologists would say, fear of failure, rejection, or success—or sometimes simply because they know someone will take care of them.

In your case, knowing we won't kick you out, you correctly assume you can continue your pleasure-centric life without much consequence. The best I can do is to ask whether you'll feel good about your life having done the least you can get away with rather than the most you could produce?

If you don't feel good about such a life, you'll have to learn to get comfortable being uncomfortable and force yourself to do the things you know you need to do: work harder to get and keep a job, even if it's not a "fun" job. Hopefully, you'll come to appreciate that you'll feel better about yourself and your life by being self-supporting, productive, and a good role model for your child. You'll also, if you wish, be more likely to meet and keep a good romantic partner. That's my best shot, Chad.

Would you have said something different to Chad?

Planner

He had it all planned out.

In high school, he did what it took to get into a designer-label college. So he took the teachers known to be an easy A, took the SAT three times to maximize his score, and chose extracurriculars mainly on how much they'd impress colleges: He played tuba in the band, rode crew, and volunteered in a homeless shelter. And he got into a designer-label college.

Knowing that prestigious medical schools prefer applicants with both research and clinical interest, he volunteered in a biotech lab in his sophomore summer and worked as a medical scribe in a hospital in his junior summer. Again, he made sure to take the easiest professors for the science courses, in which A's are key to medical school admission. And he was admitted to medical school.

Wanting a relatively low-stress worklife, he angled for and succeeded in landing a dermatology residency rather than, for example, internal medicine or oncology, let alone surgery.

He wanted to own a home and so started looking for a well-below-market-priced fixer-upper early, knowing it could take a long time to find such a home, and after a year, he did. Don hired local workers rather than contractors to do the repairs and remodeling, which saved him a fortune.

Indeed, in all ways, he kept his spending down, for example, driving an old Toyota rather than a new Beemer so he could start saving. He chose a simple but effective plan. Every time he had a $500 to invest, he wouldn't try to pick stocks let alone time the market. That day, he'd simply invest it in <u>Vanguard Growth Index Fund,</u>[18] a low-cost way of investing in a range of top companies.

He wanted a wife and children but deliberately deferred the search until his career was solidified. Then he placed a thoughtful ad on carefully selected dating websites and asked trusted friends to get set up. A year later, he was married. A year after that, he had his first child and a year after that, his second, which is all they wanted.

He set limits around work expectations so he'd leave enough time for work-life balance: family, sports, and a creative outlet, for example, learning to perform magic tricks.

Here is an entry He wrote in his journal at age 40:

I know many people who were as planful as I've been whose lives haven't worked out as well. If I could do it all over again, most of me thinks I'd be as planful. But part of me wonders what would have happened if I had---like that artist friend of mine does--more often let it flow, be open to life's serendipities.

Do you think you should be more planful or less? If so, in what way(s)?

The Wallet

I don't mind my job. Actually, I kind of like it. After all, the airport is virtually empty late at night and my job is easy: clean the restaurants' kitchens and bathrooms. Sure, when I started, I almost puked when I had to clean up after men with bad aim, not to mention when removing rat carcasses—Those $2 traps do work. If only those rich passengers knew that behind those frou-frou restaurants, rodents eat for free.

And you get to see all sorts of stuff that rushing passengers leave behind in the bathroom. An airport's johns get thousands of people sitting on the pot and when they're done, racing to get out of there, they slam on their pants and sometimes stuff falls out of their pocket. Usually it's just change but tonight there was a

---

[18] https://goo.gl/xlM6Xg

wallet, and it had $900 in it.

First, I wondered if was a TV show with a hidden camera trying to see how honest people are. Then I thought, nah, they wouldn't have a TV host hanging out at an airport at 1 AM. My next thought was, "Great! No one could prove it was their money. I could use 900 extra bucks. But then I realized that the owner could call the airport, hoping an honest person would turn it in and then, sleazo-me would disappoint them? Let me look inside the wallet. Maybe it's a tycoon's. Hmm, "Tom Michaels, consultant in employee productivity tracking." Is he one of those guys who has people like me wear FitBits connected to the corporate computer to be sure I'm not goofing off?

I thought about it as I was pushing my cart to my next stop, Bistro Alegria. (I had to pull *two* rats out of *there*.) When I was almost there, I saw a fellow cleaner and, on impulse, decided to offer her the cash and then bring the wallet with the credit cards to the lost-and-found. That way, I'd feel less guilty.

I told her where I got the money and she turned it down. "It's not your money to give."

I said, "Yeah but we're cleaning toilets for 17 bucks an hour and I'll bet he makes 10 times that selling an electronic leash to make sure we're earning our 17 an hour. Screw him. Keeping the money is just playing a little Robin Hood."

She softened a little: "Well maybe if we used it for a good cause, like donating it to an urban school for after-school tutoring?"

I reminded her that our tax dollars and rich people's donations to charity pay for all that.
She tried, "How about dividing it among all the bathroom cleaners?"

I said, "They'd want to know where the money came from. So we'd have to lie or we'd get in trouble."

She said, "Give it back."

My final shot was, "How about we keep $30 of it as a "finder's fee" and I use it to take you out for breakfast after our shift?"

She hesitated and then said, "Okay."

*I read this **on YouTube.***

"Wild Man"

"I'm sorry, Bob. It's Stage 4...There are things we can try to..."

Bob interrupted. In that instant, a lifetime of having been "nice," vanished: "Drop dead. Your false hope last time only subjected me to expensive torture: $50,000 for "chemotherapy" poison?! You doctors are pigs!"

And Bob stormed out. As he was driving home, he decided he would give his death sentence a silver lining. Now, if he felt it would do good for society, he would be completely honest. After all, what could they do to him now?

So the next night. he went to the gala fundraiser. In the middle of the pooh-bah's speech urging people to "dig deep to invest so as to finally close the achievement gap," Bob stood up in the audience and said,

Over the past half century, we've spent $22 TRIILLION[19] to try to close the achievement so-called gap, and it's nearly as wide as ever.[20] Better to spend on nurturing our best and brightest. Even if you raise $10 million tonight, it's nothing compared with the trillions we've already wasted.

And Bob strode out, followed by Derek, a blowhard who was ever insisting, "If only we did things right (his way,) we could make a big difference." Derek went into his rap and Bob interrupted: "You are far more ignorant than you think you are and if you really wanted to make a difference you'd shut up and learn the realities." And Bob strode away as Derek seethed, "You're a wild man!"

---

[19] https://goo.gl/MHcpws
[20] https://goo.gl/J2XyIM

Bob went home, turned on CNN and saw what must be the thousandths media piece on excessive force by police. He then wrote a letter to CNN:

To feel good in front of your pseudo-intellectual friends, you in the media attack law enforcement. Anyone watching would think half of cops are monsters hell-bent on shooting "unarmed black men." In your heart, you know that 99.9% of the time—often under incredibly stressful and abusive circumstances that you would crumble under—police officers do the right thing, and the people in the "community" are grateful to them. In your heart of hearts, you know that your biased reporting on the police exacerbates unfairly the mistrust between the community and the police. In your heart, you must know that your relentlessly harping on the tiny fraction emasculates the police's ability to protect the community you claim to care so much about. And deep down, you must know you're deterring would-be police officers from applying to be a cop, thereby ensuring a worse pool of police officers. If you really care about people, be honest instead of pandering to the lords of political correctness.

And while Bob was at it, he wrote another letter to the editor: "Why do you relentlessly impose a double-standard on the Israelis, who have done so much good for the world while you treat other groups with kid gloves?"

And then Bob cried, murmuring "Nothing matters."

The takeaway

Should we all be more honest? I'm honestly not sure.

Arguable

Alex always liked to argue. Of course, it started during the Terrible Twos: "No, I don't want to eat that!" "No, my sister can't have my toy!" "No, I don't want to go to bed!"

When Alex was a little older, his father told him, "A sign of intelligence is to raise smart disagreement." So even in elementary school, his hand would shoot up: "But, Ms. Johnson, isn't that wrong because…"

No surprise, Alex joined the high school debate team and, while he hated studying, the thought of "wiping my opponent's ass" made him an assiduous preparer for tournaments.

In college at Berkeley, Alex continued his, "Yes, but-ing" in and outside of class, fomenting volcanic arguments about the political issue du jour, changing few people's minds and precluding all but superficial friendships. Alex was interesting but only in microdoses.

He found a more acceptable outlet for his game by becoming an activist. At U.C. Berkeley's Sproul Plaza, speakers get on the steps of Sproul Hall and with portable PA, exhort about everything from Jesus to Palestinians, microaggressions to marijuana. If Alex wasn't on the steps, he was in the audience, salivating for the Q&A when he'd make the most skewering comment he could. When Alex finished his disquisition, how often the speaker would say, "And so what's your question?" to which Alex would respond, "What do you think of my point?" He claimed his motivation was wanting to make a difference but, in truth, it was the adrenaline rush and loving to show off his intelligence.

Of course, after graduation, Alex went to law school where, in and out of class, he lived to argue. After graduation, he took a job as an immigrant advocacy lawyer at a non-profit, where he argued fiercely for his clients as well as for liberalizing immigration policy.

He started to realize that his arguing was a net negative so he married a not-argumentative woman, and they argued rarely, although when they got together with friends, he was usually incendiary. After each get-together, he'd say things like, "I can't believe I did it again. When will I learn?" He even got to the point that before a get-together he'd rehearse to himself, "Don't argue. Better to change the topic."

One day, for no apparent reason other than the cumulative effect of his self-lectures and seeing his wife derive more benefit from her collaborative style, Alex found himself telling a colleague who started arguing with him, "You know, arguing too rarely changes people's minds. More often, it merely hardens their position. I've been fighting my whole life and I think its major impact has been to raise my blood pressure. I'm going to try to live by a no-arguing rule, replacing arguing with looking for the positive and for the opportunity to conciliate."

And from then on, Alex was far more thoughtful about when to argue. He defaulted to looking for opportunity to find common ground and, when he felt that disagreeing wouldn't too dampen the relationship, he strove to be statesmanlike.

Occasionally, Alex feels that his conciliatory behavior unduly suppresses his true nature as well as his desire to try to change the world through the clash of ideas. After all, law school taught him that's foundational to Anglo-American jurisprudence. But those doubts are outweighed by his belief that he'll probably make more change and have a more pleasant life by prioritizing collaboration over competition. But in his darker moments, he wondered whether his choice to conciliate was merely a capitulation to today's groupthink. One night as he put his head on the pillow, he thought, "They won."

The Takeaway

Do you argue more or less than you'd like? Is it time to change?

How Politicians Win

It was no surprise that Frank won the election for student body president of Ford Elementary School. Not only did his parents come up with the slogan "Frank Will Make Ford Fun," they had posters professionally designed and printed, and posted them around the school. Plus, they had taught Frank principles of winning:

- Make friends with the most popular kids and imply that if elected, you'll do them a favor.
- In campaigning, say "I'll fight for *all* students." Demonstrate that by asking them what they want from "their president" and unless it's clearly absurd, enthusiastically agree with anything they say.
- In your campaign speech, propose specific things that no one could object to: "I'll fight to get a soda machine in the cafeteria." "Stand with me again unfair report card grades."

Frank won in a landslide.

Using little more than those techniques albeit with more campaign spending, Frank became student body president of his high school and his college, then councilman, state senator, governor, and at age 63, President of the United States.

The media called him Functional Frank. Endlessly inoffensive, he had few passionate supporters but far fewer detractors. Not surprisingly, despite having served two terms as president, he could point to no major accomplishments.

After concluding his second term, he returned to his home town, where his presidential library was built. Here is the end of his dedication speech:

> I've spent my life doing what it takes to win. And I succeeded even beyond what my endlessly encouraging parents predicted.
>
> But as I sat in the back of the limo as I was driven from the White House for the last time, I finally took a step back and allowed myself to feel, to really look back at my life.
>
> And I hated myself and everything I had done. The lust for power can reduce a person to his or her worst self. I was no Hitler but I was a neutral when I could at least have been a minor force for good.
>
> So as a tiny attempt at redemption, I decided to dedicate this library to empower the people to resist people like me, other politicians like me, other salespeople like me. The Center for the Study of Manipulation will study how to arm the people—including the media—against deception and educate political, corporate, nonprofit, and government leaders to value the primacy of integrity. Indeed, integrity is all.

I apologize.

It's easy to be manipulated. Beware.

Hilda the Hypocrite

In 3rd grade, Hilda volunteered to lead her class's recycling drive. She didn't do it because she cared about the environment. She did it because she liked being in charge of *something*. She gave a speech about how "recycling can save the earth!" and kicked off the campaign by ceremoniously emptying her desk's excess papers into the recycling bin—a vivid and public but easy way to show her "commitment." That made some kids feel guilty if they threw even a tissue into the garbage can rather than into the recycling bin. Little did they know that at home, because Hilda's apartment house's recycling bin was a few steps further than the garbage bin, she'd usually toss her family's recycling into the garbage.

In Hilda's high school history class, she gave an oral report on the importance of diversity. She dug up stories of people of color being shut out and of workgroups benefiting from diversity. But when she became student body vice-president, which allowed her to pick three student senators, she chose three friends of her race and gender.

After college, Hilda took a job as an environmental nonprofit. Again, her motive wasn't to help the environment but so she could tell her friends she's working for an environmental nonprofit.

When she became her workgroup's project lead, she stressed the importance of teamwork. But in practice, she rarely pulled her weight, yet when her boss wanted pay raises to be equal for everyone in the group, she argued that she should get more because she was the project lead.

As testimony to her hypocrisy about the environment, in a Bible study class, as a Catholic, she spoke against abortion. It's tough to be an environmentalist *and* anti-abortion--Overpopulation is a leading cause of environmental degradation. Besides, she herself had an abortion!

Hilda never made much money at her job but inherited quite a chunk. She made nearly all her charitable donations, not quietly by writing a check, but at fundraising auctions, so all her friends could see her "generosity. " In fact, when she "won" an auction item, she'd usually take the full tax deduction but then resell it on eBay and pocket the cash without reporting it to the government.

When teaching Sunday School, Hilda urged her students to turn the other cheek even when the other person is wrong. Yet when driving, even when returning home from Sunday School, Hilda often gave the finger to someone who cut her off and then she tailgated him.

On Hilda's deathbed, she urged her family to work to support the environment, help the poor, and fight for the right to life. Tearfully, her family pledged to do so.

The Takeaway

Of course, many admirable-appearing people really are to be admired. But too often, even seemingly very virtuous people aren't what they seem, yet their piety can make us feel guilty and ashamed if we don't live up to their preaching and the deceptively lofty behaviors they show us. Stay alert.

Excitable Ed

From the day Ed was born, he was excitable. He popped out practically waving pom-poms.

The day his baby sister was born, he tried to dance with her.

When his preschool teacher told the class to slowly melt like ice cream cones, by the time the other kids melted, he had melted, straightened, melted, straightened, and melted again.

When he started elementary school, people didn't like that Ed was excitable:

It became a serious problem in the 2nd grade. When his teacher, Ms Tidey, asked a question, Ed would blurt out the answer. "Edward, you must wait until you're called on."

When Ms Tidey said it was time for recess, Ed raced to get a ball but Ms Tidey said, "Walk, don't run. Edward! Now you can't have a ball."

One day at recess, there were pigeons on the top of the roof. Ed kept jumping up to get a better look—until one pooped on his head. All the kids laughed at Ed.

The kids liked Ed even less than the teacher did. They would imitate Ed zooming around and they didn't even care that he saw them. The teacher once called him "Excitable Ed" and now, that's the only thing the kids called him: "Hi Excitable Ed!" "Zoom around for us, Excitable Ed!"

Still, Ed wanted to make friends so when he saw other kids giving little presents to each other, he bought a piece of bubble gum for every one of his classmates. But when he started to give them out, one child said, "That's stupid!" Another tattled to the teacher, "Ed has gum in class!" And Ms. Tidey said, "Give me that gum, Edward. Don't you know there's no gum in class?!" Ed bowed his head and gave her the gum.

Ms Tidey called Ed's mother and said, "I really think Edward should see a doctor about a Ritalin prescription to calm him down."

His mother asked, "But Ed does fine on tests, especially the standardized tests. Sure he doesn't always pay attention in class or do all his homework and it's often sloppy. But maybe if the work were harder or more interesting? Or maybe if you let him move around more?"

Ms Tidey insisted, "I think he should at least be evaluated for Ritalin."

Ed's mom said politely, "I'll think about it."

That evening at dinner, Ed asked his mom and dad, "Will the kids like me better if I take Ritalin?"

His mother replied, "Probably. And you should be able to focus better on your schoolwork."

But Ed's father asked, "Is it worth his taking uppers so he can focus on schoolwork that's too easy for him?"

His mother added, "And is it really better to homogenize our vibrant kid into just another docile one?"

Ed said: "But I want to do well in school, I want kids to like me, and I wish I could be calmer."

Dear reader, do you think Ed should take Ritalin?

Buzz

His name was Benjamin but everyone called him Buzz because he was always buzzing with energy.

As soon as Buzz hit first grade, his teacher urged his parents to have him evaluated for ADHD and Ritalin. She explained that he can get distracted by a mere bird outside the classroom window,. that he'd blurt out answers rather than wait to be called on, his desk was a mess, he'd lean back in his chair, rock, and regularly fall.

But Buzz's parents resisted because they felt the problem was mainly that school was boring, aimed at the low-achieving students. They also believed the pharmaceutical industry pushes too many kids onto Ritalin.

From the youngest age, Buzz wanted to be a doctor. So, for his birthday, his parents bought him a Visible Man model. Unfortunately, his distractibility and inability to focus caused him to lose many pieces and those he did assemble were sloppily glued because he rushed. He disliked how the model was turning out and stopped working on it. The partly completed model and box sat in his room alongside a tornado of other stuff. His parents tried relentlessly to get him to clean up his room but even on the rare occasions he did, in a week, it was back to looking post-tornado.

While Buzz wanted to be a doctor, he is an inveterate hypochondriac. Every time he got a pain of ambiguous origin, he was sure it was cancer or a heart attack. He would read article after article on health and disease but not books—They were too long for him to focus on.

In high school, Buzz's teachers agreed that he was bright and charismatic but careless and scattered. So his grades were mediocre. In college, he tried majoring in pre-med but couldn't stay focused and so switched to education.

Buzz was unable to land a job as a teacher and so became an Uber driver. Perhaps not surprising, he got into two accidents in the first few months, so they fired him.

Clueless as to what to do next, he was listening to a commercial that said that because of the teacher's strike, the school district was hiring subs at $300 a day. He got hired to sub at a tough high school.

On his first day, as Buzz approached his classroom, he saw a student's head poking out the door. Buzz nodded at him and the kid stuck his head back into the classroom and led the class in a cheer: "Sub! Sub! Sub! Sub!"

Buzz's preternaturally energized self went into overdrive. He bounced in with vibrancy and charisma the kids had never seen. And when, instead of the mandated curriculum, he improvised lessons on health, disease, and fear, including personal revelations, the class was mesmerized.

It wasn't long before the school's principal walked in. "I just wanted to see how things are going. It's awfully quiet in here." Buzz said, "I love these kids." Amazed, the principal asked the class, "Raise your hand if you think Mr. Fraser is an excellent teacher." Every hand shot up whereupon the principal said to Buzz, "Of course, you're welcome to stay through the strike, but afterwards, how would you feel about being considered for a permanent position?" Characteristically, Buzz gushed, "I'd love it. I'd absolutely love it!"

People with ADHD can thrive but only in an environment in which energy and spontaneity are helpful and in which the work day is structured in compact segments to keep the person on task. And even a personal problem, in this case hypochondria, can be used for good.

A Tough Wish Even for Santa

Dear Santa,

Sure I'd like a baseball glove but what I'd really like---and I don't think that even **you** *can get it for me—is for my class to be run by the kids.*

You see, the kids wouldn't make me sit still all day.

The kids wouldn't make me do long division when I can use a calculator.

The kids wouldn't take away our phones---They'd let us use our phones to learn with educational computer games.

I know that's a lot to ask but if you could get that for me, I'd believe in you forever and ever.

Your friend,

Matt

Matt showed the letter to his mother. She pursed her lips, "That's a tall order." Matt lowered his head and padded out. Now he was sure there really is no Santa Claus.

But his mom had an idea. She'd mail his letter to the principal. You see, Matt's mom herself was concerned that his class was poorly suited to him. In fact, Matt's teacher thought he should go on Ritalin. Maybe the letter would encourage the principal to ask the teacher to make her teaching more boy-friendly.

Christmas came and went with just the usual presents. But when Matt arrived to class on the first day of school in January, a substitute teacher was there. "I'm Mrs. Klowse. We're going to try an experiment today." Matt's eyes widened.

"We're going to let you run the class. But first, let's discuss how you'll do it. Raise your hand: Who has the first suggestion?"

Matt couldn't restrain himself and blurted out, "We'll use our phones to play educational games—Each kid can pick his own and go at their own pace!"

A few children objected, "But I don't have a smart phone."

Another student said, "I'm sure the school would buy them for you."

Matt replied, "Why don't the few kids who don't have phones share with someone they'd enjoy sharing with?"

Everyone nodded in agreement but another student asked, "What if you get stuck?"

Matt blurted again, "Then we'll ask Mrs. Klowse for help."

And so it went: an hour of suggestions, objections, and solutions. Then Ms. Klowse said, "Ready to try it?" There was unanimous assent.

The day went wonderfully and in the middle, the principal came in, watched carefully, and took notes.

It was the first time Matt could remember that he was sad when the school day was over.

But the next day, his regular teacher returned. She stood before the class and stared into the dejected kids' faces. And holding the principal's notes in her hand, she smiled for the first time ever and said, "Boys and girls...You can continue running the class."

The class cheered and Matt couldn't resist blurting out, "There *is* a Santa Claus." And from the distance, an echoey voice, "And a Mrs. Claus, I should say, Mrs. Klowse."

The takeaway

If your child is unhappy at school, would a talk with the teacher or principal be a good present?

Work

Worth

Gerald's mother sowed the seeds of her son's inflated self-confidence. "Gerald, you're so smart." "Gerald, you draw so well." "Gerald, you're so handsome." When a friend of hers asked, "How are you?" her typical answer might be, "Fine. You should see my Gerald's latest drawing!"

For a long time, other adults reinforced Gerald's high self-esteem. He got mainly A's (grade-inflated.) He suppressed thoughts about the B's and the tactfully offered "areas for growth." After school, Gerald took art lessons but his first art tutor was tough on his work so Gerald's mother replaced him with a tutor whose philosophy was "three praises for every suggestion."

Gerald wouldn't take in the less laudatory messages the world was sending him. For example, his classmates were polite to him but he got Valentine's Day cards mainly from the kids whose parents said, "Give a valentine to every child in your class." Teachers paid little attention to Gerald. When he submitted his artwork to even minor local student art contests, he usually got "honorable mention" or no response. He always managed to not let the world's indifference or negativity to him penetrate.

When Gerald applied to three art colleges and all admitted him with a "scholarship"—a one-year/no-renewal-guaranteed few thousand dollars off the $40,000 sticker price—he interpreted the admissions and "scholarship" as validation he could become a professional artist. He never realized that feedback is more credible when based not on people you're paying (like teachers) but on people who'd be paying you: customers, art galleries, etc.

Indeed, in art college, Gerald's instructors bestowed much more praise than criticism, and buoyed by that, he stayed the five years it took to finish his BFA. Now with $100,000 in student loans to pay back plus interest, he tried to sell his art, sending his online portfolio to galleries and having a booth at art fairs—Juried ones usually rejected him. Living back with his parents motivated him to "lower myself" to apply for graphic design jobs. But the best he could get was some project work, which didn't pay enough and consistently enough to afford his own apartment in the San Francisco Bay Area. So he drove a limo and worked at an art supply store near his art college, selling expensive paraphernalia to other students who dreamed of becoming professional artists, not of being deeply indebted, permanent "entry-level" workers.

Gerald's romantic endeavors were equally lackluster. He dated, but the most desirable relationships never lasted. His longest one was with Brandy who "has lots of issues." For a long time, he believed he deserved better but finally returned to Brandy and married her.

At age 40, Gerald still believed "I'm exceptional" as-is. Then he read a high school graduation speech by preeminent biographer, David McCullough.[21] Here are the key excerpts:

> None of you is special. You're not special. You're not exceptional.

> Contrary to what your soccer trophy suggests, your glowing 7th grade report card, despite every assurance of that nice Mister Rogers and your batty Aunt Sylvia, you're nothing special.

> Yes, you've been pampered, cosseted, doted upon, helmeted, bubble-wrapped. Yes, capable adults with other things to do have held you, kissed you, fed you, wiped your mouth, wiped your bottom, trained you, taught you, tutored you, coached you, listened to you, counseled you, encouraged you, consoled you, and encouraged you again. You have been nudged, cajoled, wheedled, and implored. You've been feted and fawned over and called "sweetie pie." Yes, you have. And certainly, we've been to your games, your plays, your recitals, your science fairs...

> And now you've conquered high school; and, indisputably, here we all have gathered for you. But do not get the idea you're anything special—=because you're not. Across the country, no fewer than 3.2 million seniors are graduating about now from more than 37,000 high schools. That's 37,000

---

valedictorians; that's 37,000 class presidents, 92,000 harmonizing altos, 340,000 swaggering jocks, 2,185,967 pairs of Uggs.

"But Dave," you cry, "Walt Whitman tells me, I'm my own version of perfect." "Epictetus tells me I have the spark of Zeus." And I don't disagree. So that makes 6.8 billion examples of perfection, 6.8 billion sparks of Zeus...

The fulfilling life, the distinctive life, the relevant life, is an achievement, not something that will fall into your lap because you're a nice person or mommy ordered it from the caterer.

Gerald's eyes welled up but then turned to his easel.

Is your self-esteem accurate? Is it helpful to have high self-esteem?

"Are You Going Crazy?"

For 15 years, Jonah's days were pretty much the same. He couldn't resist pushing the snooze button even though that would make him have to rush to get to work on time. And he had to leave a cushion for his unpredictable commute. Its only predictability was that it was getting ever longer—No new freeway lanes had been built nor would be, and mass transit would take much longer still.

At work, Jonah survived by working hard, not sticking his neck out, and being friendly to everyone, even to bosses he didn't like. At the end of his long workday, it was back in the car, drained, too tired to even care that the commute was ridiculous. Then it's home and to the second shift: some housework, quality time with his wife, Hannah, and the kids. Complaining would solve nothing.

Hannah worked outside the home too, so their typical dinner was a quickie salad, broiled meat, steamed veggies, and fruit for dessert—efficient but hardly inspiring. Pizza and Chinese takeout were considered treats. Then, if Jonah didn't have to tackle a honey-do list, he'd crash in front of the TV or a video game, glass of wine in hand. When his head finally hit the pillow, involuntarily, he always uttered a sigh of relief. He had made it through yet another day.

Jonah and his routine were remarkably consistent... until one night. That day was no worse than usual but he got home to find the credit card bill hadn't been paid—It had gotten buried under some papers and now there was a $75 interest charge and $35 late fee. That mote of life's realities pushed him over the edge. After Hannah said, "Don't worry about it. It's only money," he stared at her, then out the window. Thoughts of his childhood seeped in: the Crayola 64s, playing a tree in the class play, stretched out on the cool grass staring up at the clouds floating by.

After a few seconds, Hannah asked, "What are you looking at?" Jonah just pursed his lips. She hugged him but his reciprocating hug was only perfunctory.

"What's wrong?" He just stared into her eyes, impassive. Then he stared at their bedroom door, then at his kids' bedroom doors, then at the front door.

'What's wrong, honey, really? Tell me!" He couldn't make himself respond. He stared at that door for three hours.

Finally, figuring it might help if she tried to lighten the mood, she quipped, "Are you going crazy?" He kept staring.

The takeaway

Does life too-often overwhelm you? Do you have escape valves? Should you stay in lane or exit the middle-class highway, at least for a while? Is the price of a middle-class lifestyle worth it any more? Was it ever? Does another life, for example, that of the poor creative, feel wiser?

The longer I've been a career and personal coach, the more I've come to believe that other than being ethical, there are few shoulds about how to live life. How do you want to live yours?

Remaining Relevant

Nathan always loved technology, in part because it felt optimistic—Tech was always getting better. He loved technology also because he was not otherwise hip. He felt that using and talking about the latest gadgets made him nerdy-cool.

But by the time Nathan was 25, he felt like Lucy when she couldn't wrap the chocolates fast enough to keep up with the conveyer belt. The apps kept coming, the smartphone features kept coming, the media management systems kept coming. He was fighting a losing battle against younger people perceiving him as irrelevant.

In his 30s through his mid 60s, Nathan tried to stay relevant by becoming expert at his work--as a counselor specializing in adult ADHD and anger issues. He incorporated his technology interest by staying up on the latest mental health apps. He continued to stay current—doing lots of professional reading, forming a client review panel, even being watched by master practitioners.

But in his late 60s, despite all that, Nathan found his practice shrinking and, by age 70, it had dwindled to just a few clients a week. Ironically, he felt he was at the top of his game but feared that ageism was forcing him into retirement.

Nathan tried upping his marketing: calling past clients to "see how they were doing," giving talks to adult ADHD groups, and networking with lawyers who represent domestic violence perpetrators. But that merely slowed his practice's decline.

At age 72, grateful for continued good physical and mental health, Nathan found himself with too much time on his hands. So in an attempt to fill his days and to stay relevant, he applied to PhD programs. He was rejected by the accredited ones but accepted by an unaccredited one.

That program turned out to be perfect for Nathan. There were only two faculty in the department and few students, so they gave him an enormously personalized education.

He wrote his dissertation on angry people with ADHD late in life, and at age 78, completed his PhD.

Nathan converted his dissertation into a journal article read by ADHD counselors and it got reprinted in a magazine for family lawyers. Most counselors and lawyers didn't feel comfortable working with angry 70+-year-olds with ADHD, so they referred such clients to Nathan. And thus he and his practice reblossomed.

He even figured out how to incorporate his interest in technology into his work: He directed development of an app for older angry people. Nathan was now more relevant than he had ever been. He had even become a bit cool.

The takeaway

Do you need to do more to stay relevant? If so, do you know what to do? If not, do you know whom you should ask?

Workaholic or Heroic?

Even though Aaron is worth $11 million, at age 68, he continues to work 70+ hours a week, which he has done most of his life.

He does that because he believes the value of one's life is defined *totally* by how much he or she contributes to others' betterment. And while, for example, being a good family member does that to some extent, Aaron believes he makes a far greater contribution by spending all his discretionary hours building his business. He leads a small contract manufacturing firm, which takes inventors' prototypes and gets them manufactured in quantity cost-effectively, which facilitates new products coming to market, from medical devices to irrigation controllers.

Aaron married his administrative assistant in part because she shared or at least tolerated his work ethic. Grateful that child labor laws provided an exemption for family members, he had his son Joel work in his business starting at age 11.

Joel liked working in his dad's business far more than he liked school. At age 13, Joel said, "I feel like a grownup here and what I do counts. At school, I work hard on an assignment and then it gets thrown away. Here, my work helps my daddy's business."

Joel, now 40, is Aaron's vice president for operations and travels to Asia to be sure the products are consistently manufactured well and under humane conditions. Joel says he feels like a detective. "Dad warned me to be very careful. For example, sometimes, they'll show you a perfectly run factory but it's only for show. It's not really theirs—they borrow it to show American businesspeople. Or they'll do the first run beautifully—The Golden Run—and after they've gained your confidence, they'll use cheaper components, like they did with the San Francisco Bay Bridge's bolts."

Joel has become as dedicated to working long hours as is his father. One difference: Joel has decided not to marry. "I don't want to always have to apologize because I want to work evenings and weekends."

Do you consider Aaron more as a workaholic or heroic?

A Question for the Tutor

Usually, Jake tutored students who were getting C's or worse. But Darrell had gotten an A- in chemistry and his mother (more than Darrell) wanted to maximize his chances of getting into a designer-label college. So she got him a tutor, pressured him to volunteer at the homeless shelter, and to do crew—which meant waking at 4 AM to row into exhaustion in the freezing winters.

During one tutoring session, Darrell needed a break during Jake's tutoring him on—and I take this directly from the New York State High School Chemistry Core Standard 6.4.2: [22]

how dynamic equilibrium is achieved by equality of change in opposing directions, and explaining how a system returns to equilibrium in response to a stress, for example, LeChatelier's Principle.

So Darrell asked, "Jake, you know that I'm thinking about becoming a scientist. You were a scientist and left to become a tutor. What's the story?" Here was Jake's reply:

I was always good in science and math, and when my brother, who had been depressed his whole life, committed suicide while I was in college, I decided I'd become a neuroscientist and try to understand the biological basis of depression. I dreamt of finding some pill that would cure the damn thing but in graduate school, my advisor was studying how to improve electro-convulsive therapy (ECT) as a treatment for depression. To finish graduate school in a reasonable amount of time, it helped to do my dissertation on that and so I did.

---

[22] https://goo.gl/3scUak

After finishing my Ph.D., I tried to land a professorship so I could start research on finding a depression cure but even though my degree was from a brand-name university, I couldn't land even an entry-level professorship and so was forced to take a post-doc—That's a two-year low-paying research gig working under a professor. And the only post-doc I could land was related to my dissertation. ECT became a ball and chain I couldn't break from.

Anyway, I was working on a project to optimize the amount of voltage used in ECT with children. It was going well until, for a reason no one still can explain, one research subject, who was just seven years old, developed severe and permanent brain damage soon after his ECT. I was devastated and quit that day. I was virtually catatonic for a month, and afterwards swore I'd have nothing to do with biomedical research ever again.

I took a job teaching high school science but, honestly, couldn't control the class. Too many kids really didn't want to be there and didn't care if they got a bad grade, let alone whether they learned LeChatelier's Principle. So I quit with my tail between my legs and decided to tutor chemistry—One-on-one, I wouldn't have the classroom discipline problem nor the huge education bureaucracy.

Darrell asked, "So you think I shouldn't become a scientist?"

Jake sighed, "Darrell, that is such a hard question."

What do you think Darrell should do?

Unsung

Sonya always felt out of place. When her classmates were getting high on the Beatles and Stones, she was inspired by Jonas Salk and Jane Goodall.

At college, Sonya's friends were nuts over Michael Jackson, Madonna, and Prince, Mark McGwire, Jose Canseco and Roger Clemens despite their drug use. Meanwhile, Sonya was an assistant in her college's psychology research lab, studying a new kind of depression drug.

Later, her friends were gaga over, well, Lady Gaga, 2Pac Shakur, and Smashing Pumpkins, or with political candidates and their nostrums for curing all that ails. Meanwhile, Sonya was getting her Ph.D. specializing in the mathematics of the brain circuitry that's implicated in depression.

Still later, Sonya watched from afar as the public idolized the likes of Coldplay, Deerhunter, and Beyonce, who accepted $50 million from Pepsi[23] to flog sugary drinks to the very people she claims to care so much about. Other people's faves were politicians who really do lie, cheat, and steal. Or Olympic athletes who trade their childhood for Sisyphusian exercise on the very off chance they'll win some medal and soon after, almost certainly be forgotten with the rest.

Meanwhile, Sonya, working in anonymity at a research institute, while having discovered nothing, has closed some doors to curing mental illness that turned out to be blind alleys. Now, she's trying to identify biomarkers for different types of depression, each likely requiring its own circuit-level treatment. When her friends ask whether she wants to go to a party or some such, she's likely to say, "There's this research I have to finish up."

Sonya just turned 75 and decided that although she still feels productive, the lab would be better run by someone else and so she retired although she remained as an on-call advisor and mentor. Only 12 people came to her retirement party, 20 to her funeral. Sonya will indeed be forgotten with the rest.

The takeaway

Should the media be venerating different people, for example, the scientists who are extending our lifespan, who developed our iPhone, and the workaday blue-collar people who make our world run? And since the media is choosing not to do so, should we at least thank the unsung heroes in our lives? Should we not ourselves try to become one?

---

[23] https://goo.gl/AJKb1M

Facing the Music

Eli majored in his love, music composition, but also took psychology and business courses because he was urged to have a practical backup.

He played oboe in the college orchestra and became more optimistic about his musical future when one of his compositions was selected to be performed by that orchestra. He was additionally buoyed by having become first oboist in the community orchestra, which included many members old enough to be his parent.

It was there that he met and fell in love with Deborah, a violinist. Six months later, after he graduated, they married.

Her day job was in hospital administration, which made her scared of having a baby, having heard horror stories and read enough statistics to know that fear of hospitals is understandable: 400,000 people die of hospital errors annually.[24] Nevertheless, ten months later, she was pregnant.

Knowing he'd soon have to bear the financial responsibilities of fatherhood, Eli decided to be practical and back-burner his dream of a music career and instead find a way to make a living that combined his psychology and business courses.

He discovered that nearly all counseling jobs required certifications, which meant at least a master's degree plus 3,000 supervised hours. With Deborah wanting to take at least six months maternity leave and knowing that many women take-off longer or at least go part-time, he needed to make money now, not spend it on school, even if, long-term, a graduate degree might have been a worthwhile investment.

So Eli decided to try his hand at financial recovery coaching: helping spendaholics to realize that their emotional hole is unlikely to stay filled by buying "stuff." That practice's core belief is that, like other addictions, trying to buy your way to contentment is likely to result in a hedonic treadmill, spending

---

[24] https://goo.gl/ovRbBf

more and more to get that temporary shopper's high that fades ever more quickly.

Because Deborah had a rich network of friends, she helped him launch a practice that quickly generated decent income.

Alas, when Deborah went into labor a month premature, her fear of hospitals was vindicated. The nurse put epidural painkiller in her intravenous line instead of the intended penicillin for treating a labor-caused infection. The epidural drug caused cardiac arrest and Deborah and the baby died.

Eli was beyond bereft and not only cancelled all his clients but refused to see anyone for two months. During that time, he mainly stayed in his apartment and took long walks. Seeing life's transience, he decided to take a more focused stab at his dream career: music composer for films.

Knowing that was a risky goal, Eli moved to a cheaper apartment and otherwise cut his expenses. He worked six hours a day for two months to create a demo mp3 of his compositions and sent it to 20 major Hollywood film producers. He received 18 no-responses and two polite rejections, both saying that his compositions weren't good enough to yield professional employment. One of them was kind enough to say "not good enough *yet.*"

Eli deliberated whether to return to financial recovery coaching, to spend on a master's degree in music composition, or try to gain the skills on his own full- or part-time while coaching.

He decided to circle a date on his calendar nine months from that day and promised himself that he would "kill myself between now and then" to get as good as possible at composing. Living in virtual solitude, he spent most of his waking hours reading articles and books on composition, listening to Oscar-winning film scores and making notes, and incorporating everything he was learning into his own compositions.

When he feels good enough about a composition, he plans to send it to a dozen successful film composers, asking for honest feedback. It remains to be seen whether his self-imposed solitude pays off.

The Scholar

In college, when people asked Dennis why he's majoring in history, he said, "It allows me to open the curtain to an era I'll never experience." He also took many psychology courses, hoping to find help for his anxiety.

So it was not surprising that Dennis' favorite undergraduate course was History of Psychology nor that he decided to pursue a PhD in that. His dissertation was *A Comparison of Anxiety Treatment Modalities among the Post-Freudians: Horney, Jung, and Adler*. He came of age in the golden era of university hiring and so landed a tenure-track professorship.

For 34 years, Dennis did research on Freudianism, authoring 63 journal articles and four books on the subject. He taught *Intro to Psychology*, *History and Systems of Psychology*, and two graduate courses: *Freud's Legacy* and *Object Relations.* Because those fields changed little over his career, neither did his courses. When enrollment started declining, he cleverly got his courses converted from elective to required.

Finally, a new dean, a biological psychologist, asked Dennis why he refused to change with the times: "Freud is dead: His idea that our thoughts and actions are governed by an unconscious that requires years of psychoanalysis has been debunked. [25]The dean then invoked Stanford professor Ken Taylor who wrote, "There may still be a die-hard psychoanalytical cult that continues to worship at the feet of the master...But genuine scientific psychologists mostly don't take Freud seriously at all anymore."

Dennis replied, "Just because Newtonian physics has been superseded by later theories doesn't mean Newton's ideas and approaches shouldn't be studied by today's physics students. Today's physicists stand on the shoulders of giants like Newton. All your other professors are focused on what's current. But most of today's latest and greatest will end up in tomorrow's dust bin. Freud has stood the test of time and while many of his theories have been wisely disposed of, our students should understand

---

[25] https://goo.gl/GwmtID

such a giant. If it weren't for me, our students would miss that foundational learning."

That failed to convince the dean, so he decided to try to get rid of Dennis. Of course, Dennis couldn't be fired because he had tenure, so the dean made Dennis' life difficult. He "asked" Dennis to incorporate modern science research into his Introduction to Psychology course and pressured him to serve on university committees on which Dennis would do poorly. For example, in a faculty meeting, the dean said, "Dennis, we need someone with your wealth of experience on the instructional technology committee." On that committee Dennis often embarrassed himself, for example, assuming that swiping your phone refers to theft.

Beaten down, Dennis knew he needed to retire, but to extract maximum money from the university, he hired a lawyer to file a lawsuit claiming harassment and age discrimination. When the university balked, the lawyer threatened to go public: "Do you really want your donors, mostly old people, to know you're being sued for age discrimination and that you told a colleague that my client was 'Deadwood Dennis?' Some of those donors might no longer give to good ol' State U." So the university settled, giving Dennis $200,000 atop his full retirement package.

In retirement, Dennis wrote his fifth book on Freudianism.

The takeaways

Do you believe you're changing with the times as much as is wise?

Are you appropriately or excessively focused on the latest-and-greatest versus the time-honored?

If you're a student, are you taking courses required more for the professor's benefit than yours? Might you have more choice in what you take and from whom? For example, your degree-granting institution might allow you to take courses from another university or online courses from Coursera, edX, or even practical not-academic courses from Udemy, Lynda, and Udacity.

The Retirement Party

Charlie watched the clock: 4:58...4:59... 5:00. He'd finished his last day of work...forever.

What went through his mind is in *italics.*

Now's it just the retirement party and I'm out of here.

Charlie entered the cafeteria to his coworkers' applause.

Are they clapping because it's expected, in appreciation, or in appreciation I'm leaving?

At the dais, Charlie's seatmates made perky talk: "So whatcha gonna do?"

Should I be honest and admit that the first few months will be easy: clean up the apartment, read some books, take a trip, and then who the hell knows?

He said the aforementioned but omitted "and then who the hell knows?"

The emcee began with the requisite joke: "Age is an issue of mind over matter. If you don't mind, it doesn't matter."

Geez, I first heard that when I was 20. He sure didn't make much effort to prepare.

Then came the requisite exaltation: "For 35 years now, Charlie has been a fair-minded banker: meeting the needs of borrowers while protecting our depositors' money."

Big deal. Even if all our loan officers screwed up all the time, the taxpayer—the FDIC—will cover the bank's ass.

After more puffery, the emcee exclaimed, "Now, it is my distinct privilege to give you the man of the hour—well he at least deserves one hour—the man with the last name like an eye chart, Charlie Szymanszki!"

Smile more. You're trying to go out leaving a positive image. You're supposed to be gracious, even though some of members of the bank's "community," the Springfield Bank "family" weren't always so gracious. Smile, dammit!

"I want to thank you all for making Springfield Community Bank my second home."

So I'm lying but what good does it be to be honest at this point. Yeah, they can't fire me but if I say something "inappropriate," they'll think I'm going senile or something. Somehow my image here still matters to me more than being authentic.

After Charlie's speech, more small talk, dessert.

I can't wait to get out of here. I don't need to be the last one to leave. Maybe after three-quarters do.

And at that three-quarters mark, Charlie pasted on a smile, shook the hands of those he should, avoided everyone else, and strode, not trudged out.

I want them to think I'm still vital. Who knows? Maybe they'll call me back to do some consulting or something.

Charlie kept up the high-energy act as he left. Only when he closed his car door did he sigh and allow his shoulders to relax.

So, I've passed one more stop on the conveyer belt. I don't want to think of the next stop. Stop thinking about it. Think about your grandkids. I wish I were excited about seeing them more. Think about your ex-wife. I'm definitely not excited about seeing her more. Meet someone new? I still don't think I'm up for it. That's a good pun.

Charlie put the CD of the Beatles' *Help* album into his car stereo and flipped to *Yesterday*:

Yesterday all my troubles seemed so far away.
Now it looks as though they're here to stay.
Oh, I believe in yesterday.

Suddenly, I'm not half the man I used to be.
There's a shadow hanging over me.
Oh, yesterday came suddenly.

Why she had to go, I don't know, she wouldn't say.
I said something wrong, now I long for yesterday.

Yesterday, love was such an easy game to play.
Now I need a place to hide away.
Oh, I believe in yesterday.

Takeaways

Even after Charlie no longer had to fear getting fired, his desire to be perceived well still trumped his desire to be authentic. Are you more or less authentic than you want to be at work? With key people in your personal life?

Many people suppress thinking about retirement life after the first few months. After all, that's scary: Retirement is usually a one-way street to the hereafter. It's like the Roach Motel: You can check in but can't check out. How about you? Is it time to craft a first draft?

If you want to defer retiring because you'd rather work or you need the money, should you do more to boost your chances of remaining well-employed: Learn a new skill? Build your relationship with key people? Change your attitude? Work on your mental or physical health?

Thinking about retirement has the silver lining of encouraging reflection on how we want to use our limited time.

Enhance?

A May 22, 2017 New York Times headline reads: "In 'Enormous Success,' Scientists Tie 52 Genes to Human Intelligence.[26]"

A week later, the Journal of Cellullar Bioechemistry chronicled[27] the substantial progress and potential in gene editing.

Such research suggests that in a decade or three, parents may have the option of having their sperm and eggs genome-edited to ensure their child has high or at least normal intelligence.

This short-short story explores one possible implication:

---

[26] https://goo.gl/n56NDm
[27] https://goo.gl/8Kr74X

The year is 2030 and Linda and Bill are deciding whether to leave their future child's intelligence to chance or opt for genetic enhancement, which would ensure their child would have the learning, reasoning, and problem solving ability of the top 1% of the 2017 population.

Bill prefers the old-fashioned way: "I don't want to tamper with nature. With good parenting and good schools, our child will do fine. Some of society's greatest contributors weren't geniuses."

Linda disagrees: "Why saddle our child with such a disadvantage. S/he would never forgive us for making him or her go through life with a liability so difficult to overcome."

They can't agree and so decide to defer the decision until Linda got pregnant. She gets pregnant and now there is a new wrinkle: She's pregnant with identical twins. They agree on a compromise: One twin, Chip, will be genetically enhanced, the other, Dale, won't. Linda and Bob also agree they'll do everything possible to parent Chip and Dale equally.

Nevertheless, by the time Chip and Dale are three, they are markedly different. Chip is speaking in complex paragraphs, Dale mainly in single sentences. Although both go to the same preschool, Dale wants Chip to play with him: digging on the sand and rolling play doh into balls, But Chip shuns him for the advanced four-year-olds who were putting together puzzles.

After high school, Chip is admitted to United States University, America's most prestigious, run by the federal government. It spares no expense in providing the latest in education: SuperCourses, in which the student's room (at home or at the university, his choice) has four walls, ceiling, and floor covered with screens that immersed students in amazing environments: from jungles to inside a human genome to planet Mars, with learning guided by a dream team of the world's most transformational instructors. Students have to solve real-world problems in those environments. To learn needed methods and content, they just click whereupon the material is taught by one of those world-class instructors. Thus, SuperCourse students, rich and poor, from all over, receive world-class education.

Meanwhile, Dale is admitted only to Southern Arkansas State College, one of the few remaining traditionally taught colleges: a lecturer willing to live in small-town Arkansas, with discussion sections taught by graduate students.

At United States University, Chip falls in love with a fellow student, they enter into a five-year renewable marriage contract, and both are recruited by and accepted positions at Amazon.com. He is hired to improve virtual tours in Amazon's real-estate division's skyscraper department. She is hired to help develop a safer and greener flying car. They feel good about themselves and their lives, and hold off on having kids until they decide to enter into a 10-year-long child-friendly, marriage contract.

In contrast, the best job Dale can get after his six-year struggle to get a 2nd-grade teaching certificate is as a support person in an elementary school. Most elementary schools offer a scaled-down version of SuperCourses, in which there is only one live teacher per 200 students and one assistant teacher per 20 kids. The assistant's job is to show the children how to use their SuperCourse computer, troubleshoot the computer, and maintain classroom discipline. "It's a job," Dale says, "But I wish I was doing what Chip was doing and making the money he's making!"

Dale dates a number of women but can't attract someone as well-adjusted as Chip's wife. Because Dale wants children, he enters into a 20-year marriage contract but after two children and too many fights, they divorce. The divorce deepens Dale's sadness, not just because of the divorce's emotional pain but because he has to pay alimony and child support while having to live on his one modest income.

That affects Dale's work performance and a year later, he is "laid off." He tries hard to find another job but can't in education. Finally, leveraging his experience troubleshooting computers, he gets a job in McDonald's maintenance department, where he services and repairs robotic cashiers, fry cooks, and sushi makers. He feels it dehumanizing, gets dispirited and escapes with the latest designer drugs, custom-formulated to give each user a maximum high.

Alas, one time Dale has a bad trip and because he already is despondent, under the influence, he takes the laser gun that he keeps under the bed in case of an intruder, and shoots himself to death.

As Bill, Linda, and Chip trudge from the memorial service, they talk about whether it would have been wiser to have genetically enhanced Dale's intelligence? Have Chip be unenhanced?

The takeaway

Assume that at some time in the future, gene therapy will allow parents to safely ensure their children's high intelligence. Should they be allowed that option? Is that in a child's interest? The parents'? Society's?

If You Didn't Have to Work, Would You?

The year is 2050 and 2017's optimists were pretty much right: People only work if they elect to. That's because technology has made everything so inexpensive that corporate taxes can support everyone at a middle-class level.

Apartment houses are inexpensively built from an amalgam of recycled plastic and sawdust, and 3D-printed on site.

People travel mainly by solar-powered autonomous vehicles available on-demand. If only one person needs a ride between two points, a micro car arrives. If multiple people in the vicinity do, a larger vehicle is sent.

Each city is dotted with health kiosks. The person enters and makes a request. As needed, blood and urine samples are robotically taken, relevant body parts imaged, and diagnosis and medication dispensed. In ambiguous cases, an appropriate-level health practitioner (doctor, physician assistant, physical therapist, etc.,) appears on-screen to ask additional questions, remotely perform an exam, and make the diagnosis and treatment recommendation.

Amazing recreation is free. The four walls and ceiling in every apartment are covered with wall-sized TV screens. People can choose entertainment from passive TV to immersive simulations of everything from being a fetus to an intergalactic space adventure.

Education is free through graduate school because, after sixth grade, the cost per student is low: Few teachers and no school buildings are required. At home or wherever the student wishes, s/he takes highly immersive, simulation-rich courses with video explanations by the world's most transformational teachers.

Of course, some people are needed to work, for example, to create and maintain products and services. But because so much is automated, participation is voluntary, as in the 2017 military, some people elect not to work. They hang out by themselves or with friends, pursue their creative outlets, watch TV, read, or inhale custom *buzzes*, designed to give that person a maximum high with minimal side effects.

But to enhance a person's sense of self-worth and to contribute to society, most people elect to work despite no remuneration, especially those born with good intellect and drive, including the increasing number of people whose parents' elected gene editing to ensure that.

To ensure that all the world's needed work gets done, the World Government requires that people wanting to work have their brain scanned to identify the three needed jobs that best match the person's strengths and weaknesses. Each person can choose his or her favorite among their three. To ensure continuity of service and minimize the need to train more people, each worker must commit to working 40 hours a week, 48 weeks a year, for at least one year.

The takeaway

You have just been teleported to the year 2050. Do you elect to work? What, if any implications does that have for your real-life choices about your work today?

What would you imagine the brain scan would reveal to be your three greatest work-related strengths and weaknesses?

Societally, do you imagine that the freedom to elect to work would net, outweigh the decline in self-worth that accrues from more people not working?

What other consequences do you foresee from a work-optional world?

Relationships

Renouncing Sex

Few men were more sexual than him. In his college residence hall, the women quietly referred to him as Colossus, not because of his size but his ability to perform...and perform...and perform. They also loved that like other "high achievers," he was a good guy out of bed: respectful, a good listener. So, it is little surprise that he was a psychology major planning to be a therapist specializing in relationship issues.

But in his human sexuality class, he read that while the penis and clitoris have the same number of nerve endings, they're more concentrated in the clitoris.[28] That results in—all other factors equal—women experiencing more pleasure.

From then on, he noticed that his girlfriends seemed to be deriving more intense pleasure, for longer. Yes, he'd enjoy the experience and have an extraordinary few seconds at orgasm, but overall, women's pleasure seemed greater.

For a while, he rationalized that that was because he was so good and selfless in pleasuring his partners, but after having had sex with almost 20 women and been clear yet tactful to them about what he liked, he concluded women do find sex more pleasurable. He also started to realize that he was prolonging sex not to please himself but her.

Then he thought about all the romantic relationships he had had. Except for the sex, they were less pleasurable than his platonic ones or when he was doing career-related or recreational activities.

He used to think it absurd that anyone would prefer video games or basketball to sex but he started to feel that way. By the time he was 25, romantic relationships had become clearly less important to him than his career, platonic friends, and solo activities.

---

[28] https://goo.gl/43Hj4J

Then one night, after he had made particularly patient efforts to satisfy his girlfriend, he felt in need of praise after all that effort plus those growing doubts about the net benefit to him of sex. So he asked, "As they say, how was it for you?" She replied, "You really want to know?" He said, "Sure?" somehow still expecting praise. Instead she said, "I'm not sure you're equipped to satisfy me."

Shocked, without a word, he got dressed and took a long walk, at the end of which he decided to try being celibate. On his calendar, he made an appointment with himself for six months later, at which point he'd reassess.

Of course, during the six months, he was tempted to resume a sexual life, especially when meeting an attractive woman, but he somehow felt it was worth carrying the experiment to conclusion.

He had expected that as the months went on, abstinence would make him more desirous of a romantic relationship, if only out of horniness, but it was the opposite. He missed sex and romance less and less and started to feel his life was complete just with platonic friends, siblings, recreational life, and most of all, his career. He now understood why many priests, nuns, and monks claim to not miss sex.

He became a psychologist specializing in people with normal libido who chose celibacy, not because of a fear or physical problem but because they were trying to explore the wisdom of that unconventional lifestyle choice.

We all have our biases so it wasn't surprising that while he made full effort to not push clients in any direction, he, probably unconsciously, was particularly supportive of a client's desire to be celibate.

So it's ironic that after a year of that, he had a client whom, for those inexplicable reasons, inflamed him, and she returned sparks toward him. He responded appropriately: "I'm flattered that you find me attractive but it's unethical for a therapist to be romantically involved with a patient." She replied, "I heard that six months after we stop working together…"

They are now happily married.

The takeaways

How much if any of your sex life is governed not by your desire but to please your partner?

How much if any of your sex life is governed by societal expectation?

Is there anything about your sex life you'd like to change: Find a romantic partner? Not find one? Change something about the way you and your partner have sex— in frequency or the way you have sex?

Venus and Iris

Deep in the bog, with the cicadas singing, there was a flytrap named Venus.

He was just old enough to start noticing things, like that he had red traps. He thought they were ugly and wished they were green like the rest of him.

He also noticed things outside himself:

He looked to the left: Just some flytraps and some brush.

He looked to the right: Just some flytraps and some peat.

He looked ahead: Just some flytraps and lots of bog.

But then he looked behind...and *there* was an iris.

It was beautiful. It was the most beautiful thing he had ever seen.

It's hard for flytraps to talk, especially young ones, but he summoned all his energy and croaked "Hi."

Iris stared at Venus's traps and even though they were small, those teeth!

She got scared and so looked away.

Embarrassed and sad, he turned away too.

Days passed and every so often, an insect would fall into Venus's trap and as soon as it touched two of the trap's trigger hairs, the trap slammed shut. Well, a growing boy has to eat.

And the boy grew bigger. Every so often, he would look at Iris, but the bigger he got, the scarier he looked and the faster she turned away. So he did too.

Then, one day, there was loud buzzing... BEETLES!

He looked at Iris. She was *covered* with beetles! They were eating her!!

Venus widened his traps and squeezed really hard so lots of the glistening, attractive dew sat on his traps.

It worked! A beetle jumped off Iris and right onto his trap. Snap! Dinner is served.

Even though flytraps find it very hard to speak, love makes almost anything possible. So he tried to speak but alas, all that came out was digested beetle!

He tried again...more digested beetle!

He tried yet again... and finally, words came out: "Please help me save my Iris!"

But the flytraps didn't move.

"Please!," he cried.

Still the flytraps remained still.

He screamed, "I love her more than life itself!"

And that moved the flytraps. Suddenly, most of them squeezed as hard as they could. Their traps opened as wide as they could, covered with that glistening, attractive dew.

Like a magnet, the beetles jumped into the traps.

Well, most of them.

One beetle was still left on the now very wilted Iris. Now what?!

Venus couldn't eat the beetle himself. He had just eaten one and remembered what his mother had warned him: "Eat more than one a day and you'll die."

But Venus looked at Iris and he knew what he had to do. He squeezed harder than he ever had in his entire life.

Then he squeezed some more.

And all his traps opened the widest they'd ever been, even wider than you do when the doctor tells you to say "Ah!"

And all his traps were completely covered with that glistening, attractive dew.

And just like that, the last beetle jumped from Iris and into his trap. Snap!

Venus looked at Iris and he was happy.

And this time, she did not look away. She leaned toward him.

And Venus was happy..

But then Venus felt sick and he wondered, "Should I have eaten that beetle?"

The boy's red traps turned green, a sickly green.

If you were Venus, would you have eaten that beetle?

Iris knew that if she used her body to shield Venus from the sun for a day, he would live, but she, who can live only in shade, would likely die. If you were Iris, what would you do?

How much should we sacrifice for love?

Does lookism affect how much we're willing to do for others?

Are there different expectations for males versus females in this situation?

Do You Take This…?

Paula and Justin met on Coffee Meets Bagel, attracted to each other by shared interests, both having middle-income jobs, both liking to think things through, and most of all, finding each other attractive but not too attractive.

After the requisite first check-out over coffee, there was the movie date, the dinner date, then the dinner-plus-dessert date. A few months later, they moved in together and soon after, decided to marry. There was no drama, such as one person wanting to tie the knot, the other not sure. They were at the age when the peer and parental pressure plus a desire to finally be grown-ups and to have kids, all sprinkled with pixie dust, made Paula and Justin's decision a no-brainer.

Although neither Paula nor Justin were religious, they knew that at least some invitees would prefer a church wedding while even the atheists would just shrug their shoulders. So First Lutheran it was. After all, Pastor Christine had baptized Paula.

So there were Paula and Justin at the moment of truth: the vows. The pastor didn't make the mistake of rushing through the vows. She wisely allowed plenty time for the couple to let each of those time-honored phrases fully soak in.

And indeed, both Paula and Justin, consistent with their liking to think things through, reflected on each phrase:

(Paula's thoughts are in *italics*.)

"Do you Paula Whitney take Justin Novak to have and to hold from this day forward..."

"The sex is still good, although not as good..."

"For better, for worse..."

"Kathy and Tom seemed so perfect and now they're divorcing."

"For richer, for poorer,"

"What if Justin quits to work for a nonprofit?"

"In sickness and in health..."

"Mary left Charlie when his MS got bad. What would I do?"

"To love and to cherish, till death do you part?"

"Forever is an awfully long time."

After just a wisp of hesitation, to unconsciously compensate for her doubts, she exclaimed, "I do!"

(Justin's thoughts are in *italics*.)

"And do you, Justin Novak take Paula Whitney to have and to hold, from this day forward..."

I have a roving eye. I haven't cheated yet but...

"For better, for worse..."

"Peter and Trish are exhausted by their kids."

"For richer, for poorer..."

"Trish told Peter she always wanted to work but then..."

 "In sickness and in health, "

"What if Paula got cancer? What if I did?"

"To love and to cherish, till death do us part."

"Forever is an awfully long time."

Having heard Paula's hesitation, Justin too jumped right in with an assertive, "I do!"

"I pronounce you husband and wife."

Everyone applauded.

Meaning Behind the Meaning

Barbara was a psychologist who wanted to keep learning but only in bits. So she decided to improve her vocabulary. She combed advanced word lists on vocabulary.com and quizlet.com, to create a list of words she had heard of but whose meaning she couldn't recall.

She decided it might be more effective and fun to have someone test her. So she reviewed tutors' profiles on tutor.com and wyzant.com. She found herself wanting to pick an attractive man of her age who was highly intelligent, and she hit a home run: Matt has a Ph.D. in lexicography, the practice of creating dictionaries!

After just two sessions, Barbara had learned all the words on her list and didn't feel the need to unearth additional ones. But she liked working with Matt and so proposed that she and Matt have one more session, in which they'd discuss subtle differences between apparent synonyms. Barbara had an additional purpose—She wanted to seduce him. So she placed the word pairs in an order: increasingly personal.

Barbara started with, "How about 'pretentious' versus 'pompous?'" Matt replied, "The pretentious person has no basis for feeling superior while the pompous person might." Barbara replied, "So the brilliant professor diminished her appeal because of her pompous delivery, and her acolytic, sophomoric student asked a pretentious question to try to impress."

Matt said, "I'm impressed: acolytic, sophomoric? Okay, now I'll ask you one: What's the difference between complacent and complaisant?" Barbara was delighted that she knew that one: "Complacent means unjustifiably self-satisfied while complaisant means inclined to please. Here it is in a sentence: Your complaisance is mitigated by my feeling I already have a big-enough vocabulary." He smiled at her, which melted her a bit.

"Okay, Matt, here are two words that truly seem interchangeable: 'inexorable' and 'ineluctable.' Matt replied, "Few words are truly interchangeable. In this case, 'inexorable' refers to an unstoppable movement while 'ineluctable' refers to an unarguably logical conclusion. Barbara tried, "So, it's ineluctable that our inexorably plowing through my list of ostensible synonyms would come to an end, alas." She feigned a pout and he laughed.

Barbara said, "I have one more: 'salacious' vs. 'concupiscent.' Matt blushed. "That's easy: 'Salacious' refers merely to sexually oriented language. 'Concupiscent' refers to sexual desire."

And with that, their lexical relationship turned concupiscent.

Is there any unconventional way you'd like to meet someone, platonic or romantic?

Knitting

After he got laid off at age 70, he tried to find work but could get no better than a part-time, minimum-wage job as a library page.

Despite years of psychotherapy, meditation, mindfulness, and so on, he found that the only way to keep his anxiety under control was to stay busy, distracting attention from his real and imagined woes.

He was never an athlete and had no desire to, for example, take up golf, that staging area for the hereafter. Nor did he want to attend activities at the Senior Center—That would too acknowledge his place on life's conveyor belt. Watch more TV? A waste of time.

He liked to be productive but at what? He never was artsy, so other clichés were out, for example, the old man at his easel or wandering around with an outsized zoom lens, creating the zillionth image of nature's eye candy.

He flashed on his mother knitting a sweater: "Too hard." "Too feminine." "Can you just see me in a knitting circle?" So he dismissed the idea. But knitting kept intruding. "It's too hard. I'm retarded at visualizing. Maybe if it was just a scarf—that's just a rectangle, no changed angles. Maybe I should watch a YouTube video." And he did but couldn't even get the basic knit-and-purl move.

"If I took a knitting class, it would be embarrassing, not just being a man but I'd be so bad at it. Should I hire a tutor? I'm sure some little old lady would come to my house—No we'd have to meet on a park bench—She might think I'm a rapist or something."

He thought about placing an ad for a tutor on Craiglist but figured that little old ladies who knit are more likely to see an ad that was a flyer hung on some yarn store's bulletin board—if they have bulletin boards. Thorough, he went to three knitting stores. Two did have bulletin boards and the other allowed him to tape his ad to the cash register counter: "Not-so-old man, inept with crafty things, wants to see if he can learn to knit. Seeking a patient tutor: 510-122-2376."

He returned home to find a message on his answering machine— Yes, he still used an answering machine, not because he didn't understand how to set up voicemail but because he liked to screen his calls. "Hello, I'm Maudie Atkinson. The owner of A Good Yarn phoned me to say you were looking for someone to show you how to knit. You're welcome to come to my apartment."

He thought, "Well, there are four widows for every widower. Maybe she's eager. Feminist assertiveness has reached the senior set."

And so he went to Maudie's apartment, where he saw why she was so forward. She's bedridden with MS.

He was slow to pick up even basic knitting moves but Maudie was indeed patient. In showing him, increasingly, she seemed to hold his hand just a fraction of a second longer than required. And then one time, she held it for a full second. He looked her in the eye, then, reminded he was on her bed, turned away. Until once he didn't.

And he and Maudie met weekly for "knitting lessons."

Before long, he had made six scarves and sewed a label in each, "Made with love by Albert and Maudie."

The takeaway: What's an unusual way you might meet someone, romantic or platonic?

Hypochondriac

When Jeremy gets the inevitable ambiguous pains we all get, he catastrophizes into terror it's some horrible, painful, fatal disease.

He figured he could reduce his angst by marrying a physician: "Not only would I have a good doc available 24/7, with access to health care getting ever more difficult, she'd get me whatever specialists and surgery without a long delay."

To meet Dr. Right, Jeremy attended a meeting of the local medical society and even went on a continuing education cruise for doctors—to no avail. Even though he was handsome and kind, lacking the credibility of an MD degree he was a second-class citizen in single-woman docs' eyes.

Finally, he hit on a more promising approach. He submitted a proposal for a talk on fear of death and dying at the convention of the National Association of Internal Medicine Physicians. It was accepted and now, as a speaker at a week-long 10,000-doctor conference, he had credibility and the time to meet and initiate a relationship with a good internist whom he found attractive.

Indeed, he met and had a glorious few days with one, Renee. Two months later, he asked her to marry him. The proposal included admitting that while he loved her, he was also attracted to the idea of being married to a good internist as a way of easing his hypochondria.

She replied, "Alas, Jeremy, I have a bigger admission to make to you. I have cancer, stage 3. I imagine you'll want to withdraw your proposal." Driven mainly by guilt, he said, "No. I love you. Will you marry me?" Tearfully, she nodded and hugged him.

Soon after the wedding, Renee started going downhill. The disease plus the chemotherapy's side-effects made her weak, so much so that she had difficulty walking and then, even feeding herself. And Jeremy, because of his love for her and because he wanted to honor his 'til-death-do-us-part commitment, was as caring as a husband could be...for the first six months.

But then, at an oncologist appointment, with Jeremy in the room, she asked the doctor, "How long do I have?" And the physician said, "You could live a couple more years although it won't be easy years"

As Jeremy and Renee drove home, he cried, "Renee, I feel so guilty saying this but I just cannot keep doing this. I'm just 29 years old. It's been so tough just these few months and now facing two or three more years of it getting worse, I just can't." Renee replied, "I understand. I have enough money. I'll go into an assisted-living facility and my parents will help out." He said, "I'll visit you every day and help as much as I can." And he did for the three years until she died.

Even so, after she died, Jeremy remained guilt-ridden. Finally, at age 40, he thought that maybe he could find redemption by marrying someone with advanced cancer and caring for her until the end.

So he started attending cancer patient support groups until he found a woman with advanced cancer whom he found attractive. He asked her on a date. She asked, "Why would you want to go out with me?"

The takeaway

If you were Jeremy, would you have admitted to your prospective wife that one reason you wanted to marry her was that she'd provide 24/7 access to good medical care?

If you were Renee, at what point would you have admitted to Jeremy that you had stage 3 cancer?

If you were Jeremy, if Renee disclosed her cancer before you agreed to marry her, would you have married her? What if she disclosed it only after you married?

If you were Renee, would you have married him after he made his disclosure? What if he disclosed it only after you married him?

If you were Jeremy and married to Renee, would you have lived with her and been her primary caretaker for the three years until she died?

If you were Renee, at what point, if any, would you have requested assisted suicide, which is now <u>legal in a number of states and is being considered in many others?</u>[29]

The Last Taboo

Even as a teenager, he found himself less enthusiastic in bed than were his sexual partners. Even when able to get an erection, he was silent except for mild grunts at orgasm. Meanwhile, his partners would, nearly throughout, be, well, noisy.

As he got older, even in his 20s, not only did his desire decline, so did his erections. After just a month after marrying, he and his wife felt the need to go to a sex therapist. But all the exercises, analysis, and peacock feathers didn't help and she divorced him two days before his 30th birthday.

In his early 30s, he dated a number of women, hoping to find one that could sustainably turn him on, but after the first time or two with a woman, his desire waned and his fear of failure increased enough that he would break up.

---

[29] https://goo.gl/VF4oqE

He wished he were gay. That would explain the problem and provide hope that he could have a sex life. But no, he found men even less sexually attractive than women.

By his mid 30s, he decided to stop dating. He felt the pain of facing sexual failure was too great to compensate for the advantages of having a partner. Yes, he had female friends but made clear he didn't want a sexual relationship.

Through his 40s and 50s, he felt great sadness as his friends, the media, everywhere he turned, seemed to yell that the world revolved around sex and that he was being deprived of one of life's great pleasures. He, who used to be rather upbeat and at least moderately social, was getting sadder and chose to spend ever more time alone.

In his 60s and 70s, his aging increasingly beset him, which deepened his sadness and made him spend ever more time alone. He did visit porn sites but that gave him only a sliver of the sexual pleasure he imagined most of the world experienced.

Throughout his life, he felt he couldn't discuss his problem. Although people could talk about everything from group sex to S&M, no one ever admitted they had low sex drive, which is different from impotence—Not only could he not get erections, he didn't care to have them. He called low sex drive "the last taboo."

Recently however, he discovered asexuality.org, which describes itself as "The world's largest asexual community." That has brought him out of his seclusion.

Married, Filing Separately

Their marriage started traditionally: They lived together. But after three years, Laura got a great job offer requiring an hour-long commute. As an occupational therapist, good jobs are hard to find, so she took it.

Over the next few years, the commute grew even longer as the population grew but no new freeway lanes were built, so Laura decided to rent an apartment near her work to live in on weekdays.

To Laura's and Frank's surprise, they both soon preferred spending five nights a week apart. The moderately introverted Laura discovered that, after a day of having to be bubbly around her stroke and accident patients, instead of having to try to be chipper with Frank, she could unwind and recharge.

Too, they both appreciated the advantages of sleeping alone: Laura could read in bed as late as she wanted and didn't have to listen to Frank's snoring. Each could keep their bedroom at their preferred sleeping temperature. Frank could watch sports games and work in his workshop as much as he wanted without feeling guilty or getting heat from Laura to come out of his man cave.

It wasn't perfect: Frank did miss the comfort of coming home to someone. Laura missed spooning and never felt as safe in her apartment by herself. But in balance, they decided to keep the routine of five days apart, two days together.

But as time went on, the number of hours they spent together shrunk. Ever more often on a Friday night, there was some reason one of them couldn't come home. They even decided to sometimes travel separately—She loved beach vacations; he hated them. He loved adventure trips, not she.

After 11 years of marriage, Frank remains content with their increasingly separate lives but Laura has started to feel that their marriage had so eroded that she's wondering about an affair or even divorce.

Ignored

She was tired of his ignoring her.

When she wanted to discuss their sex life or lack thereof, he'd, at best, passively listen.

When Donald Trump won the presidency, she was distraught. He shrugged his shoulders.

Most painful of all, when she showed him her latest artwork, a typical response would be, "That's nice." And he'd change the topic.

Slowly, the pressure in her balloon grew. Its dénouement was triggered by the conspiring of two events. She had finished what she believed was her best and most important painting ever—a chiaroscuro of Donald Trump that made him appear preternaturally evil. Yet her husband's response was a mere, "Seems similar to something I saw before. I made a little progress today on my gene-edited cancer antigen." That brought her feeling into critical mass and into fission by her having drunk too much champagne in celebrating her having completed the painting.

She retrieved the pistol she kept under her bed in case of an intruder and with unexpected calm, shot her husband in the face. He immediately collapsed, dead. Equally unexpected, unlike in the movies, she was not horrified by her act but merely felt relief, like what we feel when clicking "send' to file our income tax return.

She coolly turned her attention to disposing of the body. Not having planned to kill him, she merely thought of what's expedient. She surveyed her house and decided to cut Jack up using his reciprocal saw and shove the parts down the garbage disposal.

She then called the police "worried" about where her husband was. The police scoured her house but she had been careful to destroy the evidence, down to flushing the disposal three times with vinegar and baking soda.

Of course, soon, friends, relatives, and colleagues frantically inquired if she had any news about Jack, and she sobbed "no."

While she had occasional flashes of remorse, her dominant feelings were of vindication and freedom. She pursued her painting as never before and even before Election Day, had completed six paintings, each using chiaroscuro to portray Donald Trump in the worst light and Hillary Clinton in the best.

She then asked a friend who owned an art gallery if she could show her collection there. She called it "Hillary and 45" in honor of U.S. Representative Maxine Waters, who refuses to call Donald Trump by his name let alone, "President Trump," but only "45."

Her friend readily agreed. The showing was a hit and boosted her art career as well as impressed her friends. "Remarkable that you were able to channel your grief into something so positive. Jack would have been so proud of you."

And all was fine until a few days later. At the junction between her house pipe and the sewer main, there was a backup. The city's sewer worker saw the source of the clog: a thick bone fragment had gotten caught in the sewer line and crud got attached to it, blocking the line. The worker thought, "That's too large for a beef bone. Hey, could this be some kind of ancient animal?" So he took it to a museum where he was informed that it was recent human bone. He then showed it to the police, which led to her arrest. Her attorney pleaded not-guilty by reason of insanity.

The takeaway

If you were the judge at her trial, are you inclined to find her not guilty by reason of insanity? Guilty? If the latter, what do you think a fair sentence would be?

Do you feel ignored by someone important? Is there anything constructive you should do about it? (Don't kill the person, please!)

Are you ignoring someone you should pay more attention to?

New Widow

They met in a psychology of personality course. Beyond being attracted to each other's looks and both being 20, they both reacted the same way to the course's concepts. For example, they nodded at Erickson's stages and Skinner's behaviorism, and giggled at Freud's concept of everyone being anal retentive or expulsive.

And they dated, lived together despite the parental opprobrium common in those days, and went on to live a conventional married life although as years went on, his career as a landscape architect plateaued while hers as a diversity trainer burgeoned.

At age 60, she was reaching her stride while he started to slow down. He began to lose hearing and energy—in and out of bed. At 70, he was diagnosed with early-stage congestive heart failure and declined until at age 75, when he had to be placed in assisted living.

At first, she was eagerly nurturing, then dutifully so, and finally, thoughts of wishing him gone intruded. First, she pushed those thoughts away but as time went on, she couldn't help thinking about what it would be like to dance again, travel again, have sex again, have good sex again. When he died, she had to admit to herself that as soon as it was socially acceptable, she would date.

And she did, younger men. First, short relationships, then a longer one, yes, with great sex. They went to Greece for an idyllic week and as they were walking hand-in-hand on the beach, they saw an old man staring into the ocean, wheezing. It reminded her of Robert. She thought,

"I know I should feel terrible that I don't think much about him, but I just don't. I didn't let him age me before my time and I feel good about that. But how could I not have felt bad that he died so much earlier than me—and his last decade was one of enervation and pain while I danced on?!"

And after an almost imperceptible sigh, she turned to her boyfriend, kissed him, and said, "Wanna find a private place on the beach?" He beamed and off they went.

The takeaway

How do you feel about her? Would you feel any different if she were a man?

In 1920, women lived only one year longer than men. The gap has grown to five years.[30] If you were a heterosexual female looking for a long-term romantic partner, should you focus on younger men? If you were a heterosexual male, should you focus on older women? What are the implications for where gender-specific health care research and outreach dollars should be spent?

---

[30] https://goo.gl/BmtGuf

Marty Nemko

Alienation

Glass Man

I could sugarcoat it and say that Clarence was "average looking." But fact is, most people consider Clarence, well, ugly.

People look through him like a pane of glass. Indeed, he called himself "Glass Man."

And when Clarence looked people in the eye, especially attractive women, they'd avert their eyes.

In retrospect, Clarence said, "I can't believe I actually did this but I was so desperate for attention, I rubbed poison oak all over my face so I'd get the sympathy vote." Not surprisingly, people were grossed out and even less likely to look at him, let alone start a conversation. He overheard one person whisper to his friend, "Do you think he has leprosy, maybe Ebola?"

And that wasn't the craziest thing Clarence did. To get attention, even though he was healthy, he told his family he had cancer. He was not a good liar, so when his family asked, "What's the course of treatments and prognosis? Can we drive you to treatments? Who's your oncologist?," his lie was quickly discovered. They yelled and yelled at him, "How dare you make us worry so much and for nothing?! Be authentic, dammit!"

So Clarence tried that. He reached out to people and said things like, "I'm lonely and vulnerable. Frankly, I'm desperate for someone to pay attention to me." In an ideal world, people would be nicer because of his desperation but, not surprising, that was as off-putting as his poison-oak-covered face.

Then Clarence figured, "Okay, I gotta fake it: Be normal. Smile more. Make small talk." And that sort of worked. People were a little nicer to him but it remained superficial. He concluded, "It's not worth being a phony when I'm getting so little in return."

So Clarence bought a solar/propane stove and heater and moved off the grid to an isolated spot near a stream in a forest outside Mendocino, California. He grew his own fruits and vegetables and drove his bike into town to pick up necessities. So he didn't need to work, he managed to get himself approved for disability: "Thank you, taxpayer!"

That lasted a year. At that point, Clarence was lonely and so took jobs in town as a house cleaner. His clients were happy with him and some conversed with him.

Like most true stories, this tale doesn't have a dramatic climax. Clarence moved into a basement studio apartment in town, made casual friends with a couple of the town's homeless people and bar denizens. He watches movies on his phone, and enjoys sunsets with his ugly dog GladWrap.

"People are a Minefield"

We live in angry times. Many people feel they must be very careful in deciding how open to be, especially about politics, let alone about race, class, or gender. In addition, the hollowing of the middle class[31] is putting ever more people on edge.

It started early. Quiet, mousy, and Christian, eight-year-old Emily was nervous leaving school each day. With reason: Often, mean boys and even girls would be waiting in the bushes outside the school, and when Emily would pass, they would pounce, force her to give them her money, or even beat her up.

That drew Emily ever more inward. She "turned the other cheek" mainly by drawing and later, painting watercolors. Her favorite subject was the Lamb of God.

Emily continued evolving her lamb paintings until she had created a series of them, some realistic, some impressionist, some abstract. But she was afraid that kids would think the paintings were bad, even make fun of her religiosity—She lived in Walnut Creek, a suburb of San Francisco in which religion is often viewed askance. So she rarely showed her paintings to anyone.

When Emily was a senior in high school, a student on the yearbook staff added three words to Emily's entry: "I'm happily pregnant." Of course, when Emily saw that, she was devastated.

---

[31] https://goo.gl/Yn5DkG

But it was too late: 1,000 copies of the yearbook had been printed and in the students' hands.

Emily chose to go to college at San Francisco State largely because it was close to home—She wanted to be able to come home for the weekends. She also chose San Francisco State—but didn't tell her parents this—because she thought it particularly likely to expose her to very different ideas. Alas, in class one day, when she quietly admitted that she was pro-life, a student ridiculed her and the professor waited a long time before saying, "That's enough." That was enough to make Emily feel she must keep her views to herself even in, maybe especially in, the so-called tolerant San Francisco.

Emily did date but chose to remain a virgin until her junior year. Her boyfriend said the he was sterile. She didn't have reason to disbelieve him, so they had sex unprotected. A few months later, she was pregnant. Disillusioned, she broke up with him. Her faith prohibited abortion and so, although she was far from ready to have a child, she had it—a difficult birth—and, after much psychological as well as physical pain, gave up her baby for adoption.

After graduating, the best job Emily could land was the 2 PM to 10 PM shift as a clerk in a county courthouse. After six months of the fatigue and impeded social life that comes from working swing shift, she got moved to the day shift. But one of the night clerks coveted that and so told the boss about a few errors Emily had made, including a serious one that Emily had covered up. The coworker said it was unfair that Emily and not he got the day shift. The coworker said that unless he got the day shift, he'd file a grievance with the union. The boss caved and moved the dispirited Emily back to the 2 to 10 shift.

Emily's upbringing taught her to value the institution of marriage. But her experiences led her to remain unmarried and to limit her contact with people. Even walking down the street, she avoided making eye contact and usually wore earbuds to signal her unavailability. She wore a gold band on the 4th finger of her left hand to make people think she's married.

Occasionally, she did date. One time, she felt comfortable enough to pull out her phone to show her date jpgs of her Lamb of God watercolors. He loved them and asked if, on his cafe wall, she'd hang his favorite: one of Jesus cradling a lamb. A few days later, he phoned to tell her that someone had splotched red paint on the lamb and, across the painting in graffiti style, scrawled "Resist!"

Emily continues to believe that gentle kindness is key to the life well-led, whether reciprocated or not. So she finds her life's main contentment in doing random acts of kindness but mainly for strangers, when it wouldn't lead to a relationship. So she feeds cars' expired parking meters when she sees a parking officer arriving. She cleans up dog droppings on the street. She volunteers in a hospital to hug abandoned newborns.

Recently, her father asked her, "You're getting ever more isolated, Emily. I'm worried about you. Shouldn't you give humankind another try?" She replied, "People are a minefield."

A Misfit Goes to a Superbowl Party

His wife dragged him to a Superbowl party. He would have rather seen a patient—He's a psychotherapist.

He knew what it would be like:

Before the game, everyone would be stuffing their face with unhealthy food and drink. He'd not have such temptations at home, but here: wings, beer, nachos.

They'd be arguing over who'll win. Who cares? The players jump to another team for an extra few bucks when they're already millionaires. If the players aren't loyal to their team why should a fan be?

Then there's the pre-game commentating—a way to stuff in more commercials, the supposed highlight of the whole extravaganza. Great: Some little ha-has to make me buy an inferior product. If it were superior, unless it was a true innovation that needed publicity, they wouldn't need to spend $1,000,000 for a 30-second ad. The 2016 Superbowl had elaborate commercials for, for example, Heinz mustard, Mini cars, Pokemon, Axe, Colgate toothpaste, and Doritos.

Then there's the game—Cro-Magnons hurling themselves against each other for four hours, the most significant results of which are concussions and permanent brain damage.

During the endless commercials, if the party guests aren't lamenting the horror of a player having dropped the ball or some such, they're boring everyone by recounting their vacation, where for thousands of dollars and massive hassle, they got to stare at a church, beach, or museum honoring the likes of King Kamehameha. Absurd.

Or they're blabbing about pop culture, fashion, gadgets, decor, restaurants, or their kids' accomplishments. Listen to the latter and you'd think we had a perfect nation: Everyone's smart, never abusing drugs, no mental illness, no laziness, no family fights. It's the in-person equivalent of Facebook, where everyone and everything is awesome.

At best, the guests are talking about who they'll vote for—based largely on Madison-Avenue-dial-focus-group-sanitized speeches (including during debates,) which are poor predictors of how effectively the candidate would run the country.

Then there's half-time and the puerile fans oohing and aahing at the changing colors, synchronized twerking and requisite political correctness: Beyonce preening atop a submerged police car and then leading her army of Black Panther-uniformed (complete with bullet bandolier) minions in a sexualized goosestep, highlighted by thrusting their fists in the Black Power salute.

By the third quarter, he told his wife, "Enjoy the rest of the Stuporbowl. I can't stand it. I'll walk home."

As he left, he turned to thinking about the clients he'd be seeing tomorrow.

Silent Scream

What might you say to this person?

She had slept badly, again. The sun just rising, she shuffled, like her patients, to the chair beside her apartment's barred window. She pulled a syringe from her robe and placed it on the windowsill.

It was the only quiet time. No roar of buses, trucks, motorcycles. No pounding of footsteps, music, or sex from her roommates nor from the adjacent apartments.

She stared out the window. Nothing, until finally, a couple sashayed by, holding hands. "They probably just slept together for the first time. A few years ago, I would have thought, 'Awww, that's sweet.' Now I think, 'Soon the infatuation may well give way to the scene in Anomalisa, where all the couple says to each other is 'Fuck you!' 'No, fuck *you*! "No, fuck *you*!' 'No, fuck *you*!'"

She had to turn away and she eyed a pile of bills: the tax bill, the huge student loan she's still paying off, the health care bill. "The health care bill—They always find a way to charge more than it should have cost even if I had no insurance. I had a stomach ache, a few tests, $800 in co-pays for $7,000 in tests that should have cost less than the co-pays. And in the end, the doctor said, 'It's probably psychological.' People shouldn't have to pay for health care. It's bad enough they're sick but to pay on top of it? To go broke on top of it? I'd be willing to be a psychiatrist for just $10 per patient visit, letting my patients supplement my income with fruits and vegetables or letting me live in their attic Actually, sometimes, I don't even believe I'm worth $10 an hour—Often, the drugs don't work well enough nor does talk therapy."

Nowhere in her pile of mail or email were responses to her job applications. "Even though I'm a psychiatrist, having given the best decade of my life to med school and residency, and paid a fortune, and being smart and persistent enough to do all that school, all I've gotten is temp fill-in work. I earned $53,000, net, last year—I can't even pay my student loan. And when I apply for real jobs, I get rejected or—more degrading—ignored. The media says that unemployment rate is 5%. That hides so much. Why does the media parrot the government's BS?"

"And we're feeling ever more inferior because of social media. Everyone's LinkedIn makes them seem like a God—"Thought leader driving change." Half the headshots are lies. It's all so demeaning, so undeservedly demeaning.

"Hi, how ya doin?" murmured the first of her roommates to awaken. She slid the syringe into her robe's pocket. 'Fine. How are you?" She thought, "What a ridiculous convention: 'Hi, how are you? Fine. How are you? Fine.' No one cares. So many people are fake, shallow, stupid or all three. And they're blank, robots, emotionless unless overreacting to microoffenses, sometimes faked overreacting: 'Would you do the dishes?'" "No! That's sexist!" Then they pick one: 'I'm offended!' 'I'm shocked!' 'I'm outraged!' Whatever happened to reasoned disagreement? Today, race and gender is a ubiquitous third rail.

"And at work, they smile to your face and stab you in the back. They want your job or just like hurting people for jealousy or sport—Yes, some people are simply sadistic. We shrinks come up with explanations that externalize responsibility: absent mother, abusive father, but some people are just mean. Others are just lazy. It's not the shit our academic professors said were the explanations: fear of failure, fear of success. Often, it *is* laziness. Yes, laziness. Charlie Kaufman is right when he wrote in *Synecdoche, New York*, 'Everyone's disappointing the more you know someone.'

"Maybe so many people are mean now because everyone's under such pressure. Good jobs are rare and if you piss off your boss, you're out. Or if you ask for too much salary, you're out. Funny, lack of competence rarely gets you fired but heaven forbid, you lose your temper once. Or you could do nothing wrong and still you're out—the boss decides the work can be done cheaper in Hyderabad.

"And where's the hope for the future? Certainly not in our future president. Clinton is a money-grubbing, divisive liar. Trump is worse—a pre-senile loose cannon. As long as big money and a four-year campaign is required to win, we'll never get candidates worthy of the world's most difficult job.

"I'm exhausted but I should get to work but, oh the commute, and after, I really need to get started on my income tax. Oh, and that credit card fraud. I gotta change my PINs. Oh and I really need to see dad." She stared through the window's bars, winced as a tricked-out Harley roared by, and trudged into the bathroom with the syringe.

The takeaway

If she were your close friend, what would you say to her or ask her about her overwhelm with modern-day pressures? About her underemployment? About her general alienation?

Any implications for you?

A Bomb

Here's how a nuclear bomb works: In an enclosed space, neutrons are shot at nuclei to break them up. When enough nuclei break up, the bomb reaches critical mass and explodes.

Adam's "nuclei" broke up easily:

In the 1st grade, he got frustrated having to wait for his turn to read. So some of his nuclei broke up.

When kids wouldn't pass him the basketball, he'd blurt, "Come on, pass me the ball!" Of course, that made kids pass him the ball less. More nuclei broke up.

Each time a girl refused to go out with Adam, more nuclei broke up.

Each time he got a B when he thought he deserved an A, more nuclei broke up.

When Adam became an architect and his job was mainly looking up code requirements rather than designing buildings, more nuclei broke up.

And when his wife left him because he wasn't sexual enough for her, lots of nuclei broke up.

Indeed, that brought Adam to critical mass. For example, around that time, he even fantasized about blowing up one of the mini-mansions he designed.

Adam lived his last years near critical mass but never blew up.

The closest he came was a deathbed letter he left for his best friend:

Dear Jamie,

I've lived a life of barely contained fury and am proud, sort of, that I never blew. Now that this may be the last time I'm coherent enough, I'd like to, unbridled, tell you why I've walked this earth so angry.

The Pretty People get such an unfair advantage. They did nothing to earn their looks yet get a huge edge in relationships and in their career. People are polite to me but never do what they do for the Pretty People.

We moderates are not embraced: If you're a hard leftist, you have your fans, if you're a hard conservative, you have your fans. But if you're a moderate, you inspire no one. Again, people are polite to you but no more. That's unfair because, in the end, Aristotle's Golden Mean has proven the wise road much more often then has radicalism.

I've killed myself my whole life to be a great architect and yet have always struggled, Yet I see far worse architects who, because they networked well or were of the right category, do better than they deserve on the merits. Nothing infuriates me as much as seeing merit increasingly taking a back seat to other factors. Not only does that unfairly injure the not-selected more-worthy people, it hurts colleges, employers, co-workers, customers, and ultimately society, all of us.

Well, I guess one thing makes me even more furious than society's often replacing merit with other selection factors: media bias. Is it that important? Yes! The media has more power to control who, what we vote for, and who gets selected, than even the reviled military-industrial complex. Because of that power, the media has a near-sacred obligation to not brainwash people but to present the full range of benevolently derived ideas, not just those ideas popular within journalists' little echo chamber. The media has become agitator-in-chief and censor of ideas that don't comport with theirs. The media does that to a far greater extent than did Joe McCarthy, whom the media continues to harp on 75 years later.

I don't feel better having unloaded on you but writing this letter feels like the most pro-social thing I can do at the end of my life. Jamie, I've made gentle efforts to discuss these things throughout my lifetime but I've been met mainly with silence, censure, and yes, damage to my career and relationships—And I wasn't brave enough to raise these issues as boldly as I have here. And to be honest, there's so much more I'd could, indeed should, say in this my last vain attempt to improve society but I'm not brave enough. But I feel I've said enough here that's worth hearing. So, Jamie, you'd do me the greatest favor if, after I die, you sent this around to folks. Thanks for considering doing that. I love you.

The Making of a Mass School Shooter

Tim seemed so normal. His parents were middle-class: an accountant and a social worker. They lived in a tract home in a middle-class neighborhood. And Tim conformed. He dressed to fit in, talked to fit in, studied only moderately to fit in.

Until high school. Then, Tim, overweight, seemed to develop breasts. One kid called him, "Tits Tim." That caught on and Tommy slowly retreated. An early sign was that he began eating lunch at the end rather than at the center of his friends' table. Then, increasingly he ate alone. At home, his former first instinct was to get together with friends, but increasingly, it was to read, watch TV, or play video games.

Tim's teachers didn't help. Dutifully, they promulgated the meme du jour: white privilege, male privilege, and their particularly despised intersection: white male privilege. And when Tim watched a sitcom, commercial, or movie, disproportionately the white male is the bad guy who is shown the way by a spunky, savvy female. (Indeed, all of the all-time top children's movies have female heroes and inferior males.[32]) Whether on tee shirts, social media, or mainstream media, the message is that the future is female, with The White Male characterized as the oppressor that has erected a glass ceiling. In short, white men suck and women and people of color are urged to fight it, loud and proud. "Wear that pussy hat!"

With his peers thinking of him as "Tits Tim" and his core influencers—teachers and the media—thinking of his race and gender as bad made Tim feel sad and angry.

---

[32] https://goo.gl/YEfDWv

The next step in Tim's dissolution was triggered by girls refusing to go out with him, the one social activity he remained eager for. The last straw was when an unpopular girl turned him down and when he asked why, she replied, "Because, well, you're Tits Tim."

Tim started to fantasize about revenge. He concocted scenarios, never thinking he'd actually do anything, but with each new scheme, he became more inured. One morning, he simply took his mom's handgun that she kept under the bed for a sense of security, walked into his first-period class and shot the teacher and four students.

The media offered various explanations: He was an entitled child, inadequate parental supervision, bullying, psychological vulnerability and most of all, guns—The politicians brayed, "We must have gun control." Tim knew that none of that was the real reason.

The takeaway

This story may be fiction but the concept is not. Despite the fact that, according to FBI and U.S. census statistics, the white murder rate is much lower than some other groups',[33] all of the major mass school shootings have been by white boys: Dylan Kleibold and Eric Harris at Columbine, Adam Lanza at Sandy Hook, Mitchell Johnson and Andrew Golden at Jonesboro, Patrick Purdy at Cleveland Elementary, Kip Kinkel at Thurston High and Charles Andrew Williams at Santana High.

What are the implications for your son of whatever race? For yourself? For schools? For the media? For the larger society?

Grumpy

It was 1:00 and Joe was about to return to the office building in downtown San Francisco where he has worked for 22 years. But today, for the first time, at age 72, he decided not to go back to work but to take the afternoon off, just because.

---

[33] https://goo.gl/zM1kqk

After phoning his boss to say he needed a few hours to himself, Joe simply started walking, taking in the sights and sounds. Here were his thoughts as he walked:

"Tattoos: Ugly defacing of the human body and it takes a year of painful treatments to undo, which may not work. So choosing to have a tattoo is usually a lifetime decision, including long after the tattoo fad has faded but the tattoo hasn't.

"Hip-hop, electronic music, modern classical music. Ugly, annoying. How can anyone like that better than _You'll Never Walk Alone_,[34] _Ebb Tide_,[35] or _The Shadow of Your Smile?_[36]"

Joe looked at the headlines at the newspaper stand. "So much emphasis on helping the have-nots. We used to call them bums, hoodlums, lazy, juvenile delinquents. Then we started to externalize their responsibility by calling them the underclass. Now we use terms that _completely_ externalize responsibility: disadvantaged, underprivileged, vulnerable, under-served. How about honoring the excellent? That's what inspires. And investing in the best and brightest is more likely to make a difference—Google, iPhone, cardiac stents—than spending yet more on the intractable underclass. In the past half-century alone, we've spent $22 trillion[37] and the achievement gap is almost as wide as ever.[38]

"So many young adults are on the streets during a weekday. I feel sorry for them. Unless you're a tech-whiz, there are fewer and fewer good jobs. And automation and offshoring can only increase. And with home prices propped up by the techno-rich and the Chinese buying up prime U.S. real estate, few young people will ever afford a home. Yet the government and media seem to pay more attention to which bathroom a transgendered person can use.

"Then there are young people I have little sympathy for. Here they are, on a Wednesday at 1:30, "protesting:" chatting and giggling with each other as they desultorily hold up a sign bearing some

---

[34] https://goo.gl/mqhGHd
[35] https://goo.gl/xULOzk
[36] https://goo.gl/yVBQ2P
[37] https://goo.gl/qPSnsC
[38] https://goo.gl/f2RhEC

bumper-sticker rhetoric. I believe they're committed to little more than not working. Their "protesting" is mainly a socially acceptable way of doing nothing other than playing with their video games, craftsy hobbies, sports, yoga mats, meditation shrines, and essential oils rather than doing what their parents and grandparents did: Do what it takes to earn a living even if it isn't "doing what you love." The vast majority of jobs are just that: jobs that make the world run. Unless you're a tech-whiz or a very talented artist or leader, no one will pay you to "follow your passion." I'm tempted to yell at them, "Earn your living—Don't be a parasite on your parents or on the taxpayer: me!

"Look at the gridlock. They want to force us out of our cars into mass-transit that sucks more hours from our already overpacked days. So they build no new freeways, convert existing ones into toll roads, turn car lanes into bicycle lanes that no one uses, and set up carpool lanes that sit underutilized because who the hell can, every day, get three people who live near you and work near you to ride with you. And so all the traffic gets compressed into fewer lanes, there's more gridlock, *more* pollution! Crazy.

"So many billboards, songs, and movies glorify casual sex. I'm no prude but is a hook-up culture really good for people? Doesn't it encourage the shallowest of relationships? Doesn't it accelerate the already lamentable decline in a couple's sexuality over time? And the marriage rate is down.[39] Can that be good for children? It's hard enough to raise a child with two parents, but with one? With revolving-door, Tinder lovers?

"And look at all those people wearing designer labels? Especially those bicyclist jerseys! How silly that people are willing to be walking billboards for corporations, which many of those people claim to hate!

"And look at all those obese people eating fast-food when there's a market selling fruit and vegetables right there! Not only are my tax dollars expected to pay for their medical expenses when they get sick, because there's a shortage of doctors, operating rooms, etc, it could cost me my life."

---

[39] https://goo.gl/OrOF2j

Joe returned home, made himself a cup of tea, sat in his easy chair, listened to <u>Frank Sinatra singing *Autumn Leaves*</u>[40] and thought, "For time immemorial, old people denigrate the next generation even though, despite retracements, things inexorably get better. I'm old. It's time to step aside."

The takeaway

If you are aging, do you want to make greater efforts to change with the times? To "rage, rage against the dying light?" Or to step aside and enjoy the timeless, simple pleasures: relationships, reading, charity, creative expression, mentoring, gardening, watching good movies and TV, nature, the arts, and spirituality?

---

[40] https://goo.gl/yCk3mM

Old Age

"My Last Concert"

In the wings, Sam could hear the concertmaster tuning up the orchestra.

"Damn, my hand is shaking more than usual—It's a bad Parkinson's day. Plus, it's my last concert—I'm nervous. Glad I decided on the Grieg, but with these hands, nothing's easy.

Sam had been a concert pianist his whole life. At age 11, he finished 4th in the Midwest Regional Young Artists Competition, and now at 83, he's performed 65 concerts, including one with the Kansas City Symphony. He thought,

"All right, that was just in the K.C. Symphony's summer festival when lots of the A players were on vacation but still...Somehow I wish my ex-wife were here. How could she have dumped me? I still wish she were here tonight...Do I play it safe? A lot of note mistakes would make the audience think I stayed at it too long, like those star baseball players who'd rather hit .200 than retire. Or do I go for a home run, a chance at a write-up in the Kansas City Star: "Roseman finishes with a flourish!"

The conductor gave Sam a forced smile and strode on stage.

"This is it. Deep breaths, deep breaths. Damn, my hands are shaking more. I'm taking too long. I gotta get out there. Stand up straight. Old men hunch. Stride, don't shuffle."

But Sam could manage only to plod on stage. He hung onto the piano with one hand as he took a modest head bow. "If I try for a full bow, I could fall."

And he sat down at the piano. "I've had this moment so many times but this is different."

Sam used his old trick of adjusting the seat up and then back down again, not because it needed adjusting but to buy a little more time to ground himself before the moment of truth.

And Sam began, and he took every not-crazy risk he could—and most of the time he won. Yes, his boldness caused a few note mistakes but only the ignorant or mean-spirited could denigrate his exciting performance. It was inspiring at any age but for an 83-year old with advanced Parkinson's?! It gives me the chills just to write about it.

And yes, Sam got not just the usual obligatory extended applause, bestowed as much to protest classical music's dying popularity as to acknowledge the performer, but fervent applause and then, yes, a standing ovation. Not a charity ovation, a heartfelt one. And Sam, who usually was too shy to really look at the applauding audience and so stared at the back wall, soaked in the smiling, standing people. Then he sighed and plodded off stage for what he thought was the last time.

Sam shuffled into his dressing room, closed the door, and dropped into a chair. "I survived. I did okay. I didn't embarrass myself, but I can't go to the reception—That's like a retirement party, where everyone tries to make light it being the beginning of the end, my end."

And then, a knock on the door. 'Daddy?" His daughter opened the door and too effusively gushed, "You were amazing. You were really amazing! Come on. They're all waiting for you."

Sam knew there was no avoiding it, so he sighed and trudged downstairs. When he arrived, the chatter resolved into applause. He thought, "I know I have to say something but I'll make it short. No one likes long speeches. And nothing ungracious. I should be a good boy."

And he began: "When we play and no one hears it, the music is incomplete. We performers are complete only with you. I am so grateful to you for making my music complete. No, my life complete."

Everyone applauded and, although Sam knew that would have been the right time to end his speechlet, the magnetism of an audience can compel a performer to keep performing. So he added, "Honestly, I can't stand the thought that this will be my last performance." And he teared up.

Just then, a four-year-old toddled up to him: "Do you want to play in my class?"

And Sam Roseman went on to play more concerts than he had in his entire life—in preschools and elementary schools, first just locally, then around the country. He never got paid, indeed had to pay all his travel expenses but didn't begrudge it: "My daughter's okay financially, so I can't think of a better way to spend my money than to teach young kids to love classical music and that old people aren't necessarily irrelevant."

The Gift

Sarah walked every hour, not because she wanted to—she hated exercise. But her doctor said, "It helps keep your circulation going." Fear of another admission to the hospital kept her padding around the block every hour, like clockwork.

Except for her walks and doctor's appointments, or should I say, physician assistant appointments, the 64-year-old Sarah rarely left home. That was such a change from having lived exuberantly until just a year ago when she had her heart scare. Her doctor insisted she was free to do anything she wanted, but her fear of death made her live over-cautiously.

Sarah was also careful about her diet—largely plant-based. She even spent the extra money on organic produce, even though that ironically could contribute to her outliving her retirement money.

Sarah did allow herself one guilty pleasure: pizza, the salt, fat, and carbs be damned. And not only pizza, but chemical-filled corporate pizza. She had a thing for Papa John's thin-crust pizza with white sauce and fresh garlic.

And Papa John's delivers. And that's what changed everything. To avoid eating Papa John's too often, she was as regimented in ordering pizza as about walking: Every other Tuesday afternoon, she'd call in her order at 4:30 so she knew she'd have her "early-bird dinner" at 5. "Bad enough to eat Papa John's, but late? I have to have some limits."

For months, Sarah had the same pizza delivery person, a well-pierced, well-tattooed, well-fed 20-year old. But one Tuesday at 5 P.M., a slender 50-year-old man showed up. He uttered the required script word-for word, "I have a small thin-crust white sauce with garlic for Sarah. Is that you?" But somehow his tone had more calm confidence than you'd expect from a pizza delivery person.

Maybe it was his tone or that she was feeling lonely, but instead of just saying, "Yes, thank you," she opened the door literally, then figuratively, "You're not my usual delivery person."

"I'm sorry..."

"Not at all. I guess also, and this probably is rude but you don't seem quite like the usual pizza delivery person."

His face dropped and she said, "I'm sorry I offended you."

"You didn't. Well, maybe a little." And a tear rose in his eye.

"I'm so sorry."

"It's nothing you did...I'm saving up for the deductible for a surgery."

Sarah couldn't resist: "What kind of surgery?"

"I should go." He started down the steps but then turned: "Kidney transplant."

To deflect the uncomfortability, she quipped, "I should give you a bigger tip."

"It's not just the money. My body needs a certain kind of donor, Type O plus the HLA allele A111."

"I don't think I can give you that."

Wryly, he waved good-bye. Sarah stared as he drove off in his rusted Toyota Tercel.

Sarah was bored with herself and her usual thoughts: fear of death, not having lived up to her potential, having remained single, not having had kids, fear of death. So she mused about donating a kidney: "My life doesn't have that much left. Even if I died from the surgery, I'd have made a bigger difference than I otherwise would. And wouldn't that be the ultimate romantic movie: We survive the surgery, get married, and live happily ever after?" On the other hand, she thought, "Are you crazy?! You were terrified of just one day in the hospital and now you're going to voluntarily spend many days there—and with major surgery?! This is all silly. You almost certainly wouldn't be a match and being in just-okay health, the doctor probably wouldn't let you be a donor."

Because of that low probability, Sarah let her curiosity outweigh her fear. At her next doctor's appointment, she asked, off-handedly, "I don't know my blood type. You said you wanted me to have another blood test anyway. How about adding blood typing."

"Sure."

"Oh and while you're at it, would you get me my HLA allele?"

"Why in the world would you want to know that?"

"Oh, it's for a genealogy thing I'm doing."

The results came back: Blood type: O. HLA allele: A111.

After a few days more of now-scary pondering, Sarah called Papa John's.

I'll spare you the painful details, but he lived...and she didn't. Her dying words, "I don't know. I just don't know."

A Journal Entry

Ever since she lost her husband, her world kept getting smaller. Now she spends most of her time walking with her cloth shopping bag to the supermarket, watching apolitical romantic movies, and cleaning her condo even if it doesn't need cleaning.

She ends most days sitting in her Stressless chair listening to the adagio movement as she sips hot chocolate even on warm nights because she and Herbie used to.

When she was motivated, she'd add a third activity to the music listening and hot-chocolate sipping: She wrote in her journal. She'd go on "runs:" For a few entries, she'd write love thoughts, then a few on aging, then a few on career. But this night, she decided to list all her dilemmas:

Should I go back to work? Back to secretarial would be easiest but something new? Scary. Am I too old to learn?

Should I date? All my girlfriends tell me to: "You're meant to be partnered." "Herbie would want you to." "I know this great, well good, guy." But the thought of taking my clothes off in front of another man...

I know I should get together more with my girlfriends. That's the problem—It's a "should." Maybe if I forced myself, it would become more of a want?

Maybe I should throw a party. But I run around like a chicken without a head and the party still comes out worse than other people's. But still...

Should I go on a cruise? Maybe a singles one? Oh, I can't resist eating. I'd gain ten pounds in the eight days, seven nights.

My belly and hips are getting bigger. Should I go on a diet again?

Maybe I should take piano lessons again. It's only been 60 years. It was so laborious. Maybe if I just tried to learn to play by ear?

Should I stop dyeing my hair? It's the only part of me that's really phony, but everyone would be shocked to see me gray. I could just see it at Christmas. The family would say, "That looks so nice" and be thinking, "God, she's aged" or "Why in the world did she stop coloring her hair?!" Maybe I should just stop wearing makeup. That's scary too.

Should I join a church? I'm such an agnostic these days, it feels hypocritical, but it did feel good to go, maybe get involved. Maybe I should go church shopping. I don't have to buy.

She ended that journal entry by writing a big question mark. Then she dug up a red sharpie and outlined it in red, closed the journal, put it in its hiding place between the water heater and its insulation blanket, and went to bed.

She awoke in the middle of the night and went on match.com.

The takeaway

Many people ruminate a lot and finally, sometimes for no ostensible reason, suddenly act. Are you ready? Should you be?

Closing

The year was 1991. Although Alex rarely made salesperson of the month, he was always at least middle-of-the-pack. But as he passed 60, his sales dwindled, and at age 70, had a heart attack and retired. The office threw him the requisite reminiscence-and-roasting party.

And Alex retreated to a life of long breakfasts, photography, and doctor's appointments. But sad at his uselessness, Alex asked his former boss if he could sit at a desk weekday mornings, when most of the agents were out prospecting or not working.

Alex showed up every morning at 9. He'd do crossword puzzles while listening to talk radio or Broadway show tunes—For his birthday, his daughter had given him a senior-friendly cell phone that she loaded with his favorite songs.

One morning, while listening to Bali Hai and immersed in the local newspaper's crossword, ("The *New York Times* ones make you know these weird words no one needs to know,") he was startled by a tap on his shoulder. It was a beautiful 25-year-old. "Hi, my name is Rebecca. Are you a real-estate agent?" His license was still active and so he nodded.

"I'm looking to buy a house but I don't know if I can afford what I want. It can be small but I grew up in an apartment that looked onto a gas station and so I'd love a view."

With the wisdom and lack of hunger that sometimes comes with age, Alex asked, "Wouldn't you be more compatible with an agent who's closer to your age?" Rebecca replied, "I've never met a salesperson who tries to talk me out of buying from him, especially a big-ticket item. You're honest, so I'd like to hire you."

That energized even the tired Alex. And he summoned every atom of energy to try to find a home that would work for her. Of course, they combed the Multiple Listings website and other online sources. Of course, he drove her to many possibilities but none worked. So then, every day, Alex spent hours, by himself, driving every block of the parts of Oakland with a view, and every time he saw a small home in bad condition (the only ones that would be affordable,) he left a hand-written note in the mailbox asking if the owner might be interested in selling.

Alex left over 100 notes, got three responses, and one was acceptable—not great—the rooms were small, only one room had a view and, as an older house, the window was small—but it was affordable—barely. To make the deal close, Alex called on lots of his old lending officers until he twisted the arm of one to not only give her a loan but at a good rate. But then the pest control report came in—$110,000! But he showed it to one of the fix-it guys he'd long used. The guy said, "Those pest control companies! I can do it for 30 grand." And so when Rebecca threw a party for her new house, Alex was the guest of honor.

But on October 19, 1991, the Oakland, California Fire Department failed to fully put out a grass fire and 2,843 single-family homes and 437 apartments and condos were destroyed---including Rebecca's.

Alex stood next to Rebecca, surveying what was left: the foundation, fireplace, and rubble. He said, "You'll rebuild." She replied, "No, *we* will."

Three years later, thanks to the insurance, Rebecca had the home of her dreams including—from three rooms—big, beautiful views.

I have lived in the Oakland hills since 1976, three blocks from the fire area. Before the fire, most of the homes were modest. The rebuilt ones are mostly mini-mansions, some not-so mini. Rather hypocritical: Nearly everyone in the Bay Area claims to be an environmentalist, yet when they got a chance to stick to the insurance companies, they built environmental monstrosities. Don King wrote, "Hypocrisy is the mother of all evil."

A Man and His Dog

Edgar is universally disliked. His co-workers view him as rigid and too judgmental. His friends largely push him away because he's argumentative and makes them feel less-than. Even his relatives minimize interaction with him.

So an ever larger part of Edgar's relationships are with his dog. Now 65, Edgar mainly hangs out with his cockapoo, Goliath: He even talks to Goliath---to talk out problems, express his frustrations with the world, speak words of love. One night he said, "Goliath, I love you so much. You're the best Goliath. I don't know how I'd cope if you died, so it would be great if we died at the same time."

Edgar's daily rituals maximally include Goliath. In the morning, Goliath wakes Edgar by kissing his face. Then, even when the Kansas winter is at its worst, Edgar gives Goliath a thorough walk. Edgar convinced his employer to allow Goliath to come to work with him. Edgar spends most of his lunch hour walking Goliath while eating a sandwich. After work, Edgar walks Goliath again, having trained him to carry the newspapers sitting in front of people's houses to their front door. When watching TV at night, Goliath lay at Edgar's feet. And of course, Goliath sleeps in the bed with Edgar—Every night there's a routine: Edgar pushes Goliath to the far corner of the bed and Goliath creeps over so he can lie against Edgar's leg. Usually, Goliath wins.

In the middle of one night, Edgar had a heart attack. Sensing something was wrong, Goliath jumped on Edgar's face and tried to help in the only way he could: licking Edgar's face, again and again. Alas, Edgar was too stricken to pick up the phone to dial 911. Suddenly, Edgar was still and Goliath returned to lie next to Edgar's leg.

In the morning, as usual, Goliath kissed Edgar's face but he didn't wake. Goliath kept kissing him to no avail and then started barking and barking. A neighbor heard it and, annoyed, called Edgar's phone number. No answer, so the neighbor, who had a key to the house, came in and saw the dead Edgar. The neighbor called the police, who took Edgar to the morgue and Goliath to the pound.

The takeaway

Put your pet in your will. Get someone to agree to care of him or her if you die. Ideally, leave some money for your pet's care. Put your will and <u>advance medical directive</u>[41] where it would be likely

---

[41] https://goo.gl/XyGXf0

seen quickly upon your death, for example, in an envelope above your bed's headboard.

Teddy

Louise had always needed alone time to recharge but rarely would say no to an invitation to a party or outing of any sort, from a half-hour hike followed by a breakfast that would add five times the calories expended, to that girls-only trip to Hawaii.

But as Louise passed 60, she slowly found herself saying no more often. She wasn't quite sure why but when she made herself get in touch with that moment of truth when she was deciding, she realized it came down to embarrassment.

She was increasingly embarrassed that at a party, she wouldn't remember the faces, let alone the names of some casual friends that, just a few years ago, she would have remembered. Worse, in conversation, she'd increasingly forget that she had told that story the last time they talked—She feared she was becoming like her father who would repeat the same story again and again.

She was embarrassed that despite eating less than she used to, her belly was getting bigger. Her daughter always praised her for not having a "mom belly." Now she had an incipient grandma belly and grandma butt. She knew it was silly to worry about such things—her weight and body shape were still at least average for her age group but she could focus only on the body she used to have. And it wasn't about attracting a guy. She decided she didn't want that. It was just for her girlfriends. Whereas she used to be slim, now she was just average. She didn't want to look like she was going to seed.

By the time Louise was 70, she had, without having made a conscious decision to become a recluse, pretty much become one. Her friends had stopped exhorting her to get together because she was unwilling to give the real reasons why she always declined their invitation.

Louise considered getting involved in the senior center activities but felt, irrationally, that that was more of a capitulation to aging than sitting holed up in her house. But that's what she did— cleaning her house daily and primping her garden as though company were coming. She did take a watercolor class but avoided interacting much with the other students. And when she concluded that she had less talent than did many of the other students, she dropped out and, to avoid competition, painted at home. Also she started keeping a journal.

Now, Louise's main company is the teddy bear she sleeps with every night.

The Oldest Bus Boy

Over his 31 years at the college's fundraising department, Harold advanced from volunteer coordinator to vice-president of human resources.

A few days after Harold's 70th birthday, his boss called him into her office. "It is incredibly difficult to say this but we need to let you go, Harold. We can get a good VP with more technical skills for much less money, which would make more funds available for programs and enable us to report lower administrative costs, which is key to getting more donations."

Remembering a line from Death of a Salesman, Harold said, "You've eaten the orange. Now you're throwing away the peel. I am not a piece of fruit!" His boss got teary but would not relent. She said, "I'm sorry. I am so sorry."

Harold's wife was completely supportive...for a month. But Harold couldn't make himself look for another job. Rather, he sat in his house—a house he now was at risk of losing—eating...and drinking...and then smoking pot, which made him eat more and care less.

Finally, his wife threatened, "Get a job...or else. I'm serious." Harold's first response was fury: "Whatever happened to 'for richer or for poorer?!'" But Harold was scared so, right away, he walked the commercial streets near his house. The only help-wanted sign in a store window was for a busboy in a chain restaurant. He went in.

The manager was legally precluded from asking anything about age but was of course wondering why a 70-year-old, well-dressed person would want a job as a bus boy, so he asked, "What makes you want this job?" Harold answered honestly, "My wife will leave me if I don't get a job and fast." He was hired. Harold said, "Maybe I should write to the Guinness Book of World's Records: The world's oldest bus boy."

Harold became a conversation piece for customers, evoking snickers among a few but more often, looks and even words of admiration. The manager even seemed to notice an increase in the number of older customers. After a month, Harold was promoted to waiter and—although it's against the law to consider age—the manager made a point of hiring an older person as a busser.

The real surprise was that Harold liked his waiter job better than his job as VP. There was a minimum of bureaucracy and he succeeded with nearly every customer, something he couldn't say about his work in fundraising. And because Harold was more thoughtful in his interactions with customers than is the typical waiter, he got excellent tips. In his first year, he earned more than $90,000.

Alas, Harold's back and knees started to bother him from standing all day, but finally, he got a bit of good luck. His manager left for a larger restaurant and Harold was offered and accepted the manager job, which didn't require nonstop standing for eight hours.

When Harold was a VP, he put in 60 hours a week, sometimes more. Now, he puts in 40 or 45 and is done, leaving time for his marriage, volunteer work tutoring low-income gifted kids, and his new hobby: using a music synthesizer to create orchestrations of his favorite melodies, which he posts as a podcast.

The takeaways

- Sometimes a serious threat is needed to break inertia.
- When adversity hits, it may be wiser to quickly get back on the bike. At least among my clients, I've found that the longer a person wallows after a setback, the harder it is to move forward.
- Even excellent employees may have to step downward but their quality quickly reveals itself and—with luck—results in renewed ascendancy.

- Up isn't the only way. Some people find greater contentment in a lower-status job.
- While age is often a minus in the workplace, it can sometimes be not just a neutral but a plus.

Seed

Emily's given name was Dakota but to channel her favorite poet, she changed it to Emily. That was but one of many things she did to amplify the muse and her identity as a poet.

Emily even poured herself into the artist's bane—marketing. Not only did she read her work at every poetry slam and open mic she could and posted her work on poetry websites, she xeroxed and later self-published collections of her poems and read them on a "portable stage:" an upside-down 5-gallon soy sauce bucket. She set up her stage mainly on Berkeley's Telegraph Ave. but also on any street with lots of lefty, literary foot traffic. And she kept producing poem after poem.

On her deathbed, Emily felt it was all for naught. Sure, a few hundred people had read or heard her work. But had any remembered any of it, let alone been changed by it? And after she died and could no longer promote her work, her impact would certainly descend from almost zero to zero.

Except it didn't quite. You see, when Brigid was 12, her mother accepted a Xerox copy of Emily's poems handed down from the soy sauce bucket. Now, 20 years later, long after Emily died, Brigid was torturing herself about whether to have a baby when Emily's poem, *From Cell to Sam: The Greatest Show on Earth,* popped into her head. She then called an international adoption agency.

The takeaway

Alas, the effect of most people's work withers but perhaps we can be motivated by the possibility that we've planted seed. Have you planted any you're proud of? Not proud of? Any you'd like to create and sow?

Bonus question: Brigid was moved to action by recalling a poem extolling the miracle of growth, from cell to person. Yet the action she chose was to go to an international adoption agency. Other than infertility, why might she have done that?

A Final Talk

Tom's father worked, slept, and then died. So did Tom, although he's not dead yet. He has Stage 4 cancer, the torture that killed his wife a few years earlier.

Tom told no one until he had to, whereupon his son, Matt, visited him in the hospital.

TOM: You didn't need to come.

MATT: Huh?! How could you not have told me you had cancer?

TOM: What good would it have done?

MATT: I'm your only living relative, dammit! The only reason I know now is that the doctor said she wouldn't let you out of the hospital until you had hospice-care set up.

TOM: How are you, Matt?

MATT: Don't change the subject. How could you not have told me?

TOM: Like I said, it served no purpose. So okay, get me hospice. I want to die at home.

MATT: Dad, what do you want to do with...

TOM: With the house and my stuff? It's all in the will. Next question.

MATT: You're no-nonsense to the end. Please, for once would you talk with me?

TOM: I'm insignificant. All I'd say was blah-de-blah blah.

MATT: Stop it.

TOM: You stop it.

MATT: Okay, we won't talk about you. Want to give me some advice or something?

TOM: Right. Deathbed advice: Okay: Work hard and use sunscreen.

MATT: Stop it! I really want to hear your best advice for me. Maybe the damn cancer is giving you more wisdom, at least more wisdom than I have.

TOM: Okay.... Accept yourself. Like me, you don't fit in. Everyone wants to change you: make you dress nicer, keep your apartment nicer, work less and be more social, make your politics more leftist, convincing you we should redirect yet more money and time from the people with the greatest potential to contribute to "the least among us." Screw 'em. In the end, they don't give a crap about you. All they really care about is to make you more like them, which makes them feel better about their pathetic conformist, hypocritical selves. In the end, you'll feel best and do best if you just keep being a free thinker.

MATT: That's an awfully lonely way to live.

TOM: It's better than being a lemming, capitulating to group-think, to ill-conceived norms created by a witch's brew of commercialism, social-science pseudo-intellectualism, and dishonest, fiscally irresponsible politicians and their media lapdogs.

MATT: I don't want to be that rejecting, that angry.

TOM: Then drop the anger but keep the integrity. If you were a lazy jerk, I'd say change, but you're neither. Oh and stop navel-gazing. More than a little introspection just gets you more mired. Turn outward. Just do good...That's it.

MATT: That's simplistic.

TOM: It's not simplistic. It's simple. And truly it all comes down to just that. Oh and hug the dog.

"Should I Kill Myself?"

He had achieved his dream of making a middle-class living as a play director. Yes, he had to live in Buffalo but there, he was in-demand as a director for semi-professional plays.

But starting in his 60s, demand for him declined such that by age 74, he had to fill his time as a model at the art school, a witness for weddings at the justice of the peace, and as a claque: someone the director plants in the audience to laugh and applaud loudly to get the audience to do so.

He also spent a lot of time thinking about The Big Issues:

Is it just to give everyone the same level of health care, whether or not they pay into the system or even whether they're in the U.S. legally? Is balance or contribution the key to the life well-led? And most recently, should he kill himself?

You see, he has cancer, stage 4, and while he has insurance to cover most of the expenses, that Big Thinker part of him asks if it's fair to society to use up so many resources to keep him alive, especially because he's weak and often in pain?

So he bought a Smith & Wesson because he heard that shooting yourself in the temple is the most foolproof and quickest way.

One day, in a moment of idealism and, okay, more pain than he had yet experienced, he pulled the gun from the cabinet, climbed into bed, threw back a shot of scotch, put on Samuel Barber's Adagio,[42] pointed the gun at his temple. and put down the gun.

He wrote in his journal,

It's easy to say what you should do. It's a lot harder to do it. And it's not just about offing yourself. We say we're going to be loving but so often we're not. We say we're going to eat less and a meal later, we're porking out. We say we'll stop procrastinating and of course we don't. So weak are we.

But I know I should kill myself. All my life I've talked about how we must, as individuals, sacrifice for the common good: be willing to take the extra time to use mass transit to do our part to stop global warming, pay our full fair share of taxes, volunteer our time to help the less fortunate, and so on. And here I am, an old dying man with crappy quality of life and little left in me to contribute,

---

[42] https://www.youtube.com/watch?v=izQsgE0L450

yet I'm sucking up probably a million dollars of precious health care resources.

A week later, he had an even worse pain episode, gulped two shots of whiskey, pulled out his gun, and put it to his head again. This time, he started to pull back the trigger, his hand shook, violently, and he put the gun down.

Two days later, he had a still worse pain jag, and it wouldn't relent. Assisted suicide is illegal in New York, so he Googled until he found the names of California doctors who routinely help terminal patients end it. And he took an Uber to the airport.

How the Earth Got Conquered in 2078

It is the year 2078 and the world has finally recovered from the so-called Viral Revolution. It started in the U.S— the inevitable explosion by The People who could no longer tolerate the mammoth and growing income inequality. Then, like a viral YouTube video, the revolution spread worldwide, even to authoritarian leviathans like China and Russia.

Now, in most countries, people are treated more equally: universal taxpayer-paid health care, transportation, housing, food, indeed all the basics, including a guaranteed basic income.

But all is not roses: People are pretty equal but can more accurately be described as equally poor. The high income tax rate combined with the relentless disparagement of society's Haves has reduced people's desire to work and to produce. So product shortages are severe and people must find their life's meaning in creative expression, relationships and, alas, drugs. Marijuana and soon hallucinogens and even opioids became legal worldwide because the few holdout countries that were worried about legalization's severe health effects were forced to capitulate as the drug-hungry populus swarmed neighborhood countries to get their chemical feel-goods, anesthetics to their life's penury.

Indeed, Adam and Sophia were high when the next Big Event started. First, they thought it was a hallucination but knew it was real when the slender, silver rocket descended onto their homette's nanofiber lawnette. A door halfway up the rocket opened and three four-inch balls, one tan, one, green, one purple, emanated and floated down onto the lawnette. Adam and Sophia crept outside to find that the balls spoke English.

The tan ball said, "We are from astral coordinates DZB, QRP, MVS, BRQ and we have received a neutrino impulse from Earth.

Sophia asked, in her stilted voice, "How do you know English?"

The green ball responded, "We all have advanced artificial intelligence. Speaking languages is nothing. We are able, in most instances, to calculate optimal individual and societal behavior."

Adam asked, "Okay, so what's the optimal societal behavior for Earth."

The purple ball said, "Our team of six, which rules our planet— That's the ideal form of government, selected by our AI system's prediction of who will do the most good for the planet—has determined that we will take over the earth."

The tan ball added, "Actually, we've already taken over. You just don't realize it yet. This week, we've released from our airborne vehicles, which are invisible to earthlings' detection systems, our Gentle Takeover Genome Replacers: Each is nano-sized so we could easily release enough to be breathed by everyone on earth three times over. For one week, you notice no changes in yourselves even though during that week, everyone's genome is slowly being replaced with ours. At the end of the week, the Replacer chemically flips a switch whereupon each earthling will start to become dramatically more intelligent, altruistic, and peaceable—You're a quite primitive civilization, actually. Frankly, it's because Earth is among the most primitive of the "advanced" planets that we decided you'd be next on our list.

Sophia exclaimed, "Next?"

The tan ball laughed. "I think we're up to about planets 4,000 by now."

Green added, "We're a little nervous about other planets taking *us* over!" We're hopeful that any planet with the AI to do that will be even more altruistic than we are—Only foolish AI would be malevolent. But who knows?"

Adam asked, "So what's going to happen to the earth after the week?"

Purple said, "Earth will slowly become like the other 4,000 planets: no more crime, no more wars, all your intelligence will cure cancer, provide good work for all, elect better leaders—We learned that your presidents have included a peanut farmer, a B actor, a sleazy businessman, and a talk show host.

Tan asked, "Her name was Opah?"

Adam said, "Not quite but I know who you're talking about. She served four terms before being replaced by Brutus, a wrestler.

The balls laughed, waved goodbye, floated up into their space needle, and it soared away.

Three years later

In Adam and Sophie's immersion room with all four walls being ultra-OLED 3D screens, they're watching the first anniversary celebration of one-world government at the United Nations. One of the world's six leaders rises to speak:

> It seems appropriate today that we look back at our accomplishments since DZB, QRP, MVS, BRQ bestowed its genome upon us. It was just three years ago yet the accomplishments, I must say, dwarf what we earthizens had accomplished in the previous 100:

> We've permanently figured out how to keep government and banks from retaking the financial system from cryptocurrencies. That keeps trillions of dollars in the people's hands.

> Our artificial intelligence system has optimized the amount of the guaranteed basic income so it still provides incentive

to work while providing life's basics to all. And our AI in-home edutainment system, with its profound understanding of how to teach and motivate people, has given nearly all our populus— with its genetically enhanced intelligence—the ability to do so many different kinds of work, all well. The System has also engendered in nearly everyone a *desire* to work—Finally, nearly everyone realizes that being productive and contributing to a better world is infinitely more important than hanging out or buying stuff.

There's no shortage of jobs any more, thanks to The System having identified so many unmet needs that people are willing to pay to get met. We're particularly proud that literally billions of earthizens are now serving as physicians, on-call when a citizen's health belt signals them. Thanks to the AI-driven Dr. Watson, Version 235.0, only six months of training is required to be an effective physician.

Because nearly all of us have a good life or the hope of attaining one, substance abuse has declined to virtually zero.

Cancer, with all its human and fiscal costs, has been eradicated and premature heart disease is on its way out.

Today's automated farming has created all the food the world needs, and in an environmentally sound way. Because of that and the brilliant insights of our genetically enhanced and AI-assisted scientists, we've harnessed nuclear energy to provide virtually unlimited green energy that's safer than fossil-fuel energy. We've stopped climate change and species degradation.

En toto, Earth's Gross Happiness Index is three times that of the highest scoring country in 2018: Bhutan.

Of course, not everything is perfect. Our edu-modules and AI-assisted legislators and judges haven't yet solved the Israeli-Palestinian conflict. And some people still complain of racism, sexism, elitism, lookism, weightism, and increasingly, demeanorism. But our enhanced genomes give all six of your leaders realistic hope that by the dawn of the 22nd century, those problems will be as solved as the problem of income inequality and climate change.

Adam said "Alexa, screens off" and all four screens faded to Navajo White.

He asked Sophia, "The president is so optimistic. Do you worry about anything?"

Sophia said, in that stilted voice of hers, "Humankind, even with its enhanced genome, has not quelled the Darwinian desire to compete, to have more than the neighbor does. War or even greed will not be permanently replaced by kumbaya and 'From each according to his ability, to each according to his need.'"

Adam didn't want to face that, so he pulled her close to him, kissed her, and Sophia opened her robot mouth to receive him.

*I read this **on YouTube.***

Made in the
USA
Middletown, DE